Teaching With Favorite Magic Tree House Books

BY DEBORAH ROVIN-MURPHY
AND FRANK MURPHY

NEW YORK • TORONTO • LONDON • AUCKLAND • SYDNEY
MEXICO CITY • NEW DELHI • HONG KONG • BUENOS AIRES

SCHOLASTIC
Teaching
Resources

We would like to acknowledge Karen Scheuer
for her great ideas and research in several
clusters of this book. Her enthusiasm and hard
work helped make this book informative,
useful, and fun. Karen is on her way
to a great writing career!

Cover from THANKSGIVING ON THURSDAY by Mary Pope Osborne, illustrated by Sal Murdocca. Jacket illustration copyright © 2002 by Sal Murdocca. Used by permission of Random House Children's Books, a division of Random House, Inc. MAGIC TREE HOUSE is a registered trademark of Mary Pope Osborne; used under license.

Cover from MIDNIGHT ON THE MOON by Mary Pope Osborne, illustrated by Sal Murdocca. Jacket illustration copyright © 1996 by Sal Murdocca. Used by permission of Random House Children's Books, a division of Random House, Inc. MAGIC TREE HOUSE is a registered trademark of Mary Pope Osborne; used under license.

Cover from BUFFALO BEFORE BREAKFAST by Mary Pope Osborne, illustrated by Sal Murdocca. Jacket illustration copyright © 1999 by Sal Murdocca. Used by permission of Random House Children's Books, a division of Random House, Inc. MAGIC TREE HOUSE is a registered trademark of Mary Pope Osborne; used under license.

☆ Contents ☆

About This Book

"My favorite book as a child was Egermeier's *Bible Story Book*, written in 1923. It's a very hard book and very long (607 pages!). But I started reading it in third grade, and I read three stories a day for several years," says Mary Pope Osborne. "Each time I finished the book, I'd start it all over again. It was a strange thing for a kid to do, but I deeply loved that book." Now Mary is the author of a series of books that millions of children will remember as a favorite. Through the Magic Tree House® series, Mary Pope Osborne has inspired millions of children to read—and keep reading!

Magic Tree House books take readers on magical journeys to the past where a pair of heroic siblings, Jack and Annie, display courage, confidence, and strength as they tackle one problem after another. What makes Jack and Annie so likeable are their ordinary qualities. They say things like "Oh, man," and "Cool," are fond of rainbows and cute animals, and enjoy joking around. And, like their young readers, they have normal fears, doubts, and questions about the world around them. Children easily connect with the Magic Tree House books. Whether children are learning about dinosaurs or dingoes, the *Titanic* or twisters, they're captivated.

What's Inside?

In the pages that follow, you'll find activities for extending the learning that comes naturally with the Magic Tree House series. Each Magic Tree House book is grouped in a cluster of four related titles. Here's a quick look at what you'll find for each cluster and individual title:

◎ **Story Summaries:** Find out fast what each book is about.

◎ **Connect the Clues:** Get a preview of how the four titles in each cluster are connected. Find out what clues lead children from one book to the next and what discoveries they'll make along the way.

◎ **Fact Finders Scavenger Hunt:** Guide children to understand how fictional characters can reveal nonfiction information with a scavenger hunt for each Magic Tree House cluster. Take the hunts further by challenging children to use resources, such as corresponding Magic Tree House Research Guides, to find out more about the information they learn. Use the activity as a springboard to reinforcing features of nonfiction, such as maps, diagrams, captions, boldface type, and glossaries.

◎ **Before You Read:** Strengthen higher-level reading skills with quick activities for introducing each book.

◎ **After You Read:** Enhance the skills and concepts children are learning in the classroom with interdisciplinary activities and games that connect events in the book to the curriculum.

- **Magic Tree House Research Guides:** Develop students' appreciation for nonfiction with these lively guides. Extension activities provide practice in taking notes, creating diagrams, constructing time lines, and more.

- **Reproducible Pages:** Reinforce skills and concepts with independent activity and pattern pages.

- **Resources:** Choose from fiction and nonfiction books, as well as Web site suggestions, to support a Magic Tree House study. (See pages 15–16.) Please check Web sites in advance, as locations and content may change over time.

Tip

The official Magic Tree House Web site offers comprehension questions, discussion topics, news, and author comments. You can even join the Magic Tree House Club for e-mails about upcoming books and related activities! Go to Random House Books:

www.randomhouse.com/ kids/magictreehouse

Tips for Teaching With a Series

Teaching with a series enriches learning in many ways. Many teachers rely on using a series such as the Magic Tree House books to increase children's interest in reading regularly. Reading books in a series can help readers take risks with more difficult text because they have familiar "friends." These friends are the characters, the plot, and the author's style. Having familiar characters allows readers to make more accurate predictions: they can anticipate what characters will do based on other books. Familiar plot devices assist readers in summarizing information, drawing conclusions, and making inferences. An author's recognizable style brings a level of comfort to the reading experience, and it allows readers to more fully focus on the story.

Teaching with a series can help children become stronger writers as well. While different elements, such as character, setting, and goal may vary, the basic plot structure often remains the same. Young writers can apply familiar patterns to their own writing as they experiment with story structure. Even writers who have difficulty organizing and planning a writing piece can use the patterns from the Magic Tree House books to create their own story. By substituting their own setting, goal, and characters, students have a scaffold on which to build their story.

Of course, anticipation for what the next book in the series will bring is one of the strongest motivators, and a great reason to use a series in the classroom! Following are tips for teaching with the Magic Tree House series:

- To accommodate developing readers, provide multiple copies of each title so children can follow along in their own book as you read aloud.

- Recorded readings of the books are helpful when students are absent or when they need to reread text for better understanding. If there are no commercial recordings, invite the principal or school volunteers to record the book on tape.

- Have a classroom celebration after completing each cluster. Display maps, projects, pictures, and any other artifacts created during the cluster study. Students will feel a sense of accomplishment as they revisit the four books they've read, and they'll eagerly look ahead to the next set.

- Invite students to create book clubs with classmates so they can support each other in reading books that are not read aloud by the teacher.

Connections to the Language Arts and Social Studies Standards

The activities in this book are designed to support you in meeting the following standards outlined by the Mid-continent Research for Education and Learning (McREL), an organization that collects and synthesizes national and state K–12 curriculum standards.

Language Arts

Uses the general skills and strategies of the reading process and uses reading skills and strategies to understand and interpret a variety of literary texts.

◆ Previews text (for example, skims material, uses pictures, textual clues, and text format)

◆ Establishes a purpose for reading (for example, for information and for pleasure)

◆ Makes, confirms, and revises simple predictions about what will be found in a text (for example, uses prior knowledge and ideas presented in text, illustrations, and titles)

◆ Knows setting, main characters, main events, sequence, and problems in stories and, in third grade, understands the basic concept of plot (for example, main problem, conflict, resolution, and cause and effect)

◆ Knows the main ideas or theme of a story and, in third grade, understands elements of character development in literary works

◆ Makes connections between characters or simple events in a literary work and people or events in his or her own life

Uses reading skills and strategies to understand and interpret a variety of informational texts.

◆ Understands the main idea and supporting details of simple expository information

◆ Knows the defining characteristics of a variety of informational texts (for example, textbooks, letters, diaries, and directions)

◆ Uses text organizers (for example, headings and graphic features) to determine the main ideas and to locate information in a text

◆ Uses the various parts of a book (for example, index, table of contents, glossary, appendix, preface) to locate information

◆ Summarizes information in texts (for example, includes the main idea and significant supporting details)

◆ Uses prior knowledge and experience to understand and respond to new information

Uses the general skills and strategies of the writing process.

◆ Uses prewriting strategies to plan written work (for example, uses graphic organizers, story maps, and webs; groups related ideas; takes notes; brainstorms ideas; organizes information according to type and purpose of writing)

◆ Uses strategies to organize written work (for example, includes a beginning, middle, and ending; uses a sequence of events)

◆ Writes in a variety of forms or genres (for example, friendly letters, stories, information pieces, responses to literature) and for different purposes (for example, to inform, learn, and communicate ideas)

◆ Writes in response to literature (for example, summarizes main ideas and significant details; supports judgments with references to personal knowledge)

Gathers and uses information for research purposes.

◆ Uses a variety of sources to gather and plan research and information (for example, informational books, pictures, charts, indexes, and Internet)

◆ Uses multiple representations of information (for example, maps, charts, photos, diagrams, tables) to find information for research topics

◆ Uses strategies to gather and record information for research topics (for example, uses graphic organizers and summarizes information)

◆ Uses strategies to compile information into written reports or summaries (for example, incorporates notes into a finished product; includes simple facts, details, explanations, and examples; draws conclusions; and uses appropriate visual aids)

Uses listening and speaking strategies for different purposes.

◆ Makes contributions in class and group discussions (for example, reports on ideas and personal knowledge about a topic, initiates conversations, connects ideas and experiences with those of others)

◆ Uses level-appropriate vocabulary in speech (for example, words that describe people, places, things, events, location, and actions)

Social Studies

Understands selected attributes and historical developments of societies in Africa, the Americas, Asia, and Europe.

◆ Understands the main ideas found in folktales, stories of great heroism, fables, legends, and myths from around the world that reflect the beliefs and ways of living of various cultures in times past

◆ Understands the daily life, history, and beliefs of a country as reflected in dance, music, or the other art forms (such as paintings, sculptures, and masks)

◆ Knows significant historical achievements of various cultures of the world (for example, the pyramids in Egypt and bookmaking in China)

Understands family life now and in the past, and family life in various places long ago.

◆ Knows the cultural similarities and differences in clothes, homes, food, communication, technology, and cultural traditions between families now and in the past

Understands how democratic values came to be, and how they have been exemplified by people, events, and symbols.

◆ Understands how historical figures in the U.S. and in other parts of the world have advanced the rights of individuals and promoted the common good and the character traits that made them successful (for example, persistence, problem solving, moral responsibility, respect for others)

Source: *Content Knowledge: A Compendium of Standards and Benchmarks for K–12 Education* (3rd ed.). Mid-continent Research for Education and Learning, 2000.

Meet Mary Pope Osborne

What do students want to know about the author of the Magic Tree House series? Share the questions and answers below to learn more about this favorite author and her work.

Deborah Rovin-Murphy and Frank Murphy: Of all the locations and time periods in the series, which would you most like to travel back to and why?

Mary Pope Osborne: I would most like to travel back to the time of Shakespeare. In *Stage Fright on a Summer Night*, Jack and Annie go to Elizabethan England, 400 years ago, and meet the playwright William Shakespeare. I can't imagine anything more exciting than that.

DRM and FM: Who are you most like—Jack, Annie, or Morgan le Fay?

MPO: I'm a little like Jack, in that I love to read and gather knowledge. And I'm a little like Annie in that I'm very emotional and love animals. I'm a little like Morgan le Fay, too, in that I love to turn kids on to reading and using their imagination.

DRM and FM: Are there any places/time periods/events you want to write about that you haven't yet included in the series?

MPO: There are lots of people, places, and times I still want to write about: the great painters of the Renaissance; the musician and composer, Mozart; the island of Hawaii long ago; Mount Everest; penguins in Antarctica; nomadic life in the desert. The list is long.

DRM and FM: What is your first memory of wanting to be a writer?

MPO: When I was growing up, I had no idea that I could ever be a writer. I thought only brilliant, special people could be writers, not ordinary people like me. Not until my late twenties did I even begin to imagine I might find a place for myself in the world of writing books.

DRM and FM: If you had to name three favorite Magic Tree House books, which would they be?

MPO: At this moment (and this could change tomorrow), my three favorite Magic Tree House books are *Ghost Town at Sundown*, *Civil War on Sunday*, and *Polar Bears Past Bedtime*.

DRM and FM: Any secrets, interesting anecdotes, or hints about the series you can pass along?

MPO: I wrote many, many, many first drafts of the very first Magic Tree House book. I tried to get two kids back in time in so many different ways. None of them worked. I tried having the kids blow magic whistles, visit a magic museum, meet a magic painter. I wrote seven different books, using seven different ways to make the magic happen. Nothing seemed to be working. Then one day I was taking a walk with my husband in the country, and we saw a kid's tree house, an old, falling-down tree house. As we were looking at the tree house, the idea for the magic tree house "took root." It was a simple answer to a very complicated process. But often I find simple solutions take a long time to uncover.

Photo: Paul Coughlin

Teaching Activities
for Any Time

In addition to the activities suggested for each Magic Tree House cluster and title, try any of the following ideas to enrich your students' learning experiences with the series.

Tip

▲▲▲▲▲

Write Your Own Adventure

Students can use what they learn about the patterns in the books to write their own Magic Tree House adventures. To generate an idea bank, brainstorm places or time periods that have not been explored in the series and think about how Jack and Annie could find an adventure there! For related writing activities, see Tree House Titles (page 13), More Great Adventures (page 12), Building a Mystery (page 24), and The Best Beginnings (page 52).

Plot Passport

(Language Arts and Social Studies)

A passport is like a ticket to another country. It is also a record of where you've traveled. Jack and Annie not only "travel" around the world, they also travel back in time. With their predictable patterns and familiar characters, Magic Tree House books help readers develop a sense of story structure. Use a passport format to explore these patterns. Give each child a copy of the passport on page 17 as you introduce each new Magic Tree House book. Have children cut out the four passport pages and staple them together. Invite students to gather the necessary information as they read to complete each page in the passport. Once they've traveled around the Magic Tree House world, they can use O-rings to bind each set of passport pages for a record of their reading success.

Words to Know (Language Arts)

Magic Tree House books are rich with content-area vocabulary. Some of these words may be unfamiliar to students. Help students build meaning (and vocabulary) as they read by completing a Words to Know chart for each book. Photocopy the chart on page 18 and make a master by filling in vocabulary words from the book. Before reading a book, students can write definitions for words they know, and check the appropriate column for other words. As they read, this will help cue them to words they don't know and encourage them to use reading skills and strategies to find out the meaning.

Make a Map (Social Studies and Language Arts)

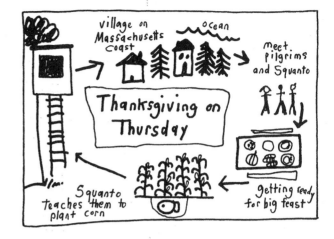

In each Magic Tree House book, Jack and Annie travel outside of Frog Creek, Pennsylvania—to places as far away as the Wild West in *Ghost Town at Sundown* to the Great Plains of Africa in *Lions at Lunchtime*. Let children deepen their understanding by making maps to go with the books they read. Creating a map of a story builds skills on many levels. For starters, it deepens children's appreciation of the setting, encouraging them to notice details of time and place. Mapping the setting also helps children focus on sequence and use logical thinking skills. Encourage children to label each part of their maps.

Traveling Through Time (Math and History)

The Magic Tree House series covers history from prehistoric times to present day. Make a series time line that covers all the books from the earliest to the latest time period.

◎ Divide the class into small groups. Assign each group a Magic Tree House cluster.

◎ Have students in each group make a list of the titles in their cluster and the approximate time period.

◎ Bring students together and, using each group's information, put the series in chronological order. Have students create a large time line with the information, recording book titles and dates in the corresponding positions. As they read each book, they can add illustrations to the time line to represent significant details.

Getting to Know Jack and Annie (Language Arts)

Jack and Annie bring two unique perspectives to the story line in each Magic Tree House book: Jack is mostly interested in the facts, while Annie is mostly interested in the adventure. When Annie's adventurous nature gets the kids into trouble, Jack's research skills help them figure out practical solutions. Challenge children to find evidence to support their differences in each book. Encourage children to notice other characteristics, too. Display a life-size cutout of each character. On the cutouts have children record information about each character as they read. Use the information children gather to discuss how Jack and Annie's personality traits both help them and hinder them at times.

Tip

Students can use their maps as a guide to retell the stories, building an understanding of story structure and a familiarity with the adventure genre.

Meet Morgan le Fay (Language Arts)

With each title in the series, Jack, Annie, and readers learn more and more about the mysterious owner of the tree house, librarian Morgan le Fay. Help students keep track of what they learn by creating an "All About Morgan" poster. After reading each title, have students record new details about the magical librarian. (For example, she travels through time, she's mysterious, and she has a soft voice.)

Story Sacks (Language Arts and Art)

Each time period and setting that Jack and Annie visit contains unique artifacts. Invite students to learn more about the details that bring each story to life by making story sacks for each Magic Tree House book. For each story sack, students will need a small brown grocery bag, art materials, pictures, and found objects. To make a story sack, have students revisit the book and list objects that are specific to the story's setting. Have them gather the objects or make pictures of them, place them in the bag, and label the bag with the title. For example, a story sack for *Day of the Dragon King* might contain a piece of silk, toy soldiers, toy horses, a picture of the Great Wall of China, a round hat made from the bottom of a paper cup, a drawing of a dragon, and a piece (or picture) of bamboo.

Comparing Fiction and Nonfiction (Language Arts)

One of the biggest reasons teachers and parents find the Magic Tree House series so enticing is that it gets students interested in history and science by introducing nonfiction information wrapped up in exciting adventures. The companion Magic Tree House research guides take the adventures further, by exploring the facts behind the fiction. Make Venn diagrams to compare Magic Tree House books with their companion research guides. What features do they have in common? How are they different?

Jack's Journal, Annie's Diary
(Language Arts and Social Studies)

To reinforce the differences between fact and fiction, make a class journal (Jack's) and a class diary (Annie's). As children read each story, invite them to record entries in both the journal and the diary. Share the entries, letting children take turns reading aloud from each book. Discuss how children determined in which book to record information—for example, facts are in boldface type so would be recorded in Jack's journal.

Tip

You might assign pairs of students to create a story sack for each Magic Tree House title. Set aside an area of the classroom to display story sacks as children complete them. Encourage students to revisit the story sacks as they continue to read books in the series to compare the setting from one book to another.

The Jack Files

(Language Arts, Social Studies, and Science)

Magic Tree House Research Guide: Space features a section called "The Jack Files." In keeping with Jack's interest in the facts, these pages at the back of the book share facts about stuff kids might want to know, like whether there is life anywhere in the universe besides Earth. Have students create "The Jack Files" for books in the Magic Tree House series, focusing on facts that are most unusual, interesting, or amazing. Bind pages in a book so that students can revisit the nonfiction information in these books and notice how their writing grows from the beginning of the series to the end.

Favorites Graph   (Math and Language Arts)

To encourage children to revisit stories they've read and make comparisons, keep a Favorites Graph throughout the series. Once children have read a few books in the series, invite them to vote on a favorite. Make a Favorites Graph to record their opinions. Include all Magic Tree House titles on the graph so children can collect and graph new data with each new book they read. Let children place a removable graph marker above the title of their favorite book. Do this each time they complete a new book in the series. (Encourage them to give reasons for their choices.) Look for patterns in the data students collect with each new graph. Are any titles always on top? Or do new stories become new favorites?

In the News   (Language Arts)

Encourage nonfiction writing skills by letting children "report" on a Magic Tree House adventure.

- ◉ Use newspaper articles to teach related skills, such as using a headline and date line. Guide children to understand the purpose of each.

- ◉ Read aloud an age-appropriate news story. As you read, have children listen for answers to predictable questions, including who, what, when, where, why, and how. Discuss how providing this information in a news article is helpful to readers.

- ◉ Let children use the newspaper article as a model for reporting "news" from a Magic Tree House adventure. Write the six questions (who, what, when, where, why, and how) on the chalkboard as a reminder for students to provide complete information.

Tip

Students might also be invited to deliver their news stories orally, as reporters on a news program.

More Great Adventures (Language Arts)

Invite students to write their own Magic Tree House adventures. To get them started, share a mini-lesson on developing characters for adventure stories. To begin, ask students to tell ways in which they are like Jack and Annie. Guide them to notice the ordinary characteristics of even heroic characters. To develop their own characters, have students answer these or other questions:

- Does your hero carry a backpack? If so, what's in it?
- What does your hero hope to have for lunch (breakfast, snack, or dinner)?
- What book could your hero be found reading?
- What part of the newspaper does your hero like to read first?
- If you looked under your hero's bed, what would you see?
- How does your hero like to get from one place to another?
- What is something your hero might think but not say?
- If your hero had a pet, what would it be?

Adventure Interviews (Language Arts)

Strengthen literal and inferential comprehension by inviting students to conduct interviews with characters from Magic Tree House stories. Students will enjoy playing the role of a journalist or talk show host as they interview Jack or Annie following one of their great adventures. Whether they're playing the part of the interviewer or the character, children will need to prepare by becoming thoroughly familiar with the characters, setting, and plot.

Write a Letter (Language Arts and Social Studies)

Letter writing is a real-life skill that strengthens voice and encourages creativity. Invite students to write letters from their point of view about events in the story. (This is a challenging exercise, as it requires children to "insert" themselves in the story and look at events from a different perspective.) Encourage students to think about which events in the story would make a good letter (or postcard). Promote literal comprehension by having them expand on their ideas with details and facts from the story. Keep this activity going by setting up a small postal center in the classroom with a supply of envelopes, paper, plain stickers, markers, and art supplies.

Tree House Titles (Language Arts and Art)

What do many of the titles in the Magic Tree House series have in common? Let children examine the titles and make a guess. (Many of the titles combine time and place—for example, *Afternoon on the Amazon, Midnight on the Moon,* and *Tonight on the Titanic.*) Invite students to come up with their own Magic Tree House book titles by combining time and place words. For example: *After Dinner in the Antarctic, Dawn in the Desert,* and *Fifth Inning in Phoenix.* Have each student create a book cover on an 8- by-10-inch sheet of paper. Display book covers on a bulletin board titled "Our Magic Tree House Adventures."

Research Guide Writers (Language Arts, Social Studies, Science, and Art)

Many of the Magic Tree House books have companion research guides. For those that don't, have students create them! Use published research guides as models, noticing features such as maps, diagrams, captions, boldface print, and indexes. As a class, determine the chapter topics. List features to include, such as maps, charts, photos, diagrams, and tables. Discuss the way the research guide authors use boldface type, captions, and other tools to assist readers. To write the guide, divide the class into small groups. Assign each a chapter. Students can work together to create a contents page, glossary, index, and so on.

Learning in a List (Language Arts, Social Studies, and Science)

Encourage students to revel in all they've learned through the series by making a topic list that starts with the first book and continues through the last.

◎ Post a sheet of mural paper labeled "Learning With Magic Tree House Books."

◎ Starting with the first book in the series, let students take turns recording all the topics they've learned about (dinosaurs, ancient Egypt, medieval times, the Revolutionary War, space, endangered species, and so on).

◎ Students can add to this list as they read each book, or use it to revisit and review all of the books when they complete the series. Either way, by the time students reach the last title, the list is sure to be impressive, and will inspire continued confidence in reading!

Five More Quick-and-Easy Ideas

KWL Chart: Introduce each book with a KWL chart. This scaffolding tool helps prepare children for reading new text, encouraging them to make connections between the subject matter of a book and what they already know. Activating this prior knowledge (and building a common background base for all students) helps children make sense of what they're reading. After sharing the title and discussing the setting pictured on the cover, invite children to share what they know (K) about the place, time, or subject matter. Record what children want to learn (W), and, after completing the story, what they learned (L).

Ask "Why?" Children are known for asking "Why?" There's a good reason for that: asking "Why?" helps them understand their world. Help them apply the same kind of thinking to the books they read to further understanding of characters, their actions, and how both help build a plot. As children read books in the Magic Tree House series, stop them along the way to ask "Why?"

Clue Countdown: After children have read at least a few Magic Tree House titles, challenge them to a Clue Countdown. Give them one clue at a time about one of the books they've read (but don't name the book). How many clues will they need to guess the title? Have children write their guesses on paper so that everyone has a chance to guess.

Connection Detectives: Invite students to be detectives, scouting out connections among books they read. For example, what people, places, or events do some books have in common? (See Making Connections, page 64, for examples.)

True or False? Reinforce what children learn by letting them create True or False quizzes to share with the class. Have them write five statements that relate to a book on index cards, and record the answers and any necessary supporting information on the back (such as the corresponding page number). Collect students' quizzes and share a few questions at a time with the class to test their Magic Tree House memories. (The quizzes students write are also a good assessment of their own understanding of the material.)

Resources

Cluster 1

Books

Eyewitness Books: Knights by Christopher Gravett (Knopf, 1993): From castles to the Crusades and Heraldry to hawking, this book offers a comprehensive and colorful history of knights.

Pirates: Raiders of the High Seas by Christopher Maynard (Dorling Kindersley, 1998): This nonfiction easy-reader is packed with colorful illustrations and photos.

Web Sites

Discovery Channel Dinosaur
www.discovery.com/area/specials/ gobi/gobi1.htm

Plug in the school's zip code to find out which dinosaurs existed in your neighborhood!

Discovery Online
www.discovery.com/stories/history/ pirates/pirates.html

Look here for photos of an expedition that may have recovered Blackbeard's ship, *Queen Anne's Revenge*.

Heraldica
www.heraldica.org

Annie would love to know that there really were women knights! This Web site is full of information about women knights in the Middle Ages.

MummyTombs.com
www.mummytombs.com

Check here for articles, recent news, photos, book recommendations, and more about mummies.

Cluster 2

Books

Journey Through Japan by Richard Tames (Troll, 2001): Informative illustrations and photographs lend support to the text in this introduction to Japan.

One Giant Leap: The Story of Neil Armstrong by Don Brown (Houghton Mifflin, 2001): Eye-catching illustrations help tell the story of Neil Armstrong, from his childhood to his first steps on the moon.

Samurai Castle by Fiona MacDonald (Peter Bedrick Books, 2001): Learn how Samurai castles were constructed and who lived in them.

Web Sites

NASA
www.nssdc.gsfc.nasa.gov/planetary/ lunar/apollo_11_30th.html

Get the Apollo 11 story, from launch to splashdown.

Ninja Kids
www.winjutsu.com

Learn more about Ninjutsu positions and Ninja history.

The Rainforest Action Network Kids Corner
www.ran.org/kids_action

This informative site features a rain forest slideshow, and detailed fact sheets with color photographs and a glossary of terms.

Zoom Dinosaurs
www.ZoomDinosaurs.com/subjects/ mammals/Iceagemammals/shtml

This illustrated site features lots of easy-to-read facts about Ice Age animals.

Cluster 3

Books

African Animals by Caroline Arnold (William Morris and Company, 1997): Fun facts, such as "If you were a giraffe, you would be able to see into a second-story window!" help students relate information about animals to their own lives.

Rhyolite: The True Story of a Ghost Town by Diane Siebert (Clarion, 2003): From the first prospectors in 1904 to a deserted town, this book explores how boomtowns became ghost towns.

Web Sites

The American West
www.americanwest.com

Learn about pioneers, cowboys, Indians, the Alamo, Buffalo Bill, and more.

Animal Populations
www.bergen.org/AAST/Projects/ ES/AP/africa.html

Learn about endangered animals of Africa, such as the Nile crocodile, mountain gorilla, and leopard, and view movies of them in action.

Cluster 4

Books

The Great Wall by Elizabeth Mann (Mikaya Press, 1997): Beautiful illustrations help tell the history of the Great Wall.

Look What Came From China by Miles Harvey (Orchard Books, 1999): Learn about inventions, foods, sports, holidays, and customs that originated in China.

Web Sites

Chinese for Kids

www.gigglepotz.com/china.htm

Students can send a Chinese New Year e-card, find their name in Chinese, or make a Chinese lantern.

Elementary Themes Viking Ships

www.stemnet.nf.ca/CITE/
vikingships.htm

Learn about different kinds of Viking ships and find links to related sites.

Nova Online: The Vikings

www.pbs.org/wgbh/nova/vikings/
runes.html

This site lets visitors type in their name to see it in runes.

Cluster 5

Books

Dingoes by Victor Gentle and Janet Perry (Garth Stevens, 2002): Colorful illustrations and photos add to this informative book.

Outside and Inside Kangaroos by Sandra Markle (Antheneum, 1999): Stunning photographs support information about kangaroos, including their life cycle, eating habits, and habitat.

Web Sites

Gulf of Maine Aquarium

octopus.gma.org/space1/titanic.htm/

Trace the *Titanic*'s route, plot wreckage coordinates on a map, use percentages to calculate lifeboat capacity, and more.

National Geographic Kids

www.nationalgeographic.com/ngkids/
9609/titanic.hml

Investigate primary resources with a survivor's true story of her experience on the *Titanic*.

Cluster 6

Books

George Washington and the General's Dog by Frank Murphy (Random House, 2002): Anecdotal stories bring George Washington to life.

Pink Snow by Jennifer Dussling (Grosset & Dunlap, 1999): From frogs raining from the sky to twisters lifting houses, this easy-reader will capture students' attention.

Red Legs by Ted Lewin (HarperCollins, 2001): Follow the footsteps of a drummer boy on the front lines of the Civil War. The surprise ending is unforgettable.

Web Sites

CyberSleuthKids

cybersleuth-kids.com/sleuth/
History/US_History/Civil_War

Photos, time lines, and other materials teach about Civil War battles, food, maps, people, and music.

Museum of the City of San Francisco

www.sfmuseum.org/1906/06.html

A time line, newspaper clippings, police and fire department reports, and photos further understanding of the San Francisco earthquake.

Tornadoes.com

www.tornadoes.com

This comprehensive site offers facts about tornadoes, tips for how to watch for them, photo galleries, lists of historic tornadoes, links to weather news, and more.

Cluster 7

Books

Hawaii Is a Rainbow by Stephanie Feeney (University of Hawaii Press, 1985): Photographs grouped by color explore food, dress, people, and flowers.

If You Sailed on the Mayflower by Ann McGovern (Scholastic, 1993): A question-and-answer format makes it easy for students to research specific information.

Koko–Love! Conversations With a Signing Gorilla by Francine Patterson (Dutton, 1999): Color photographs show Koko using signs with another gorilla.

William Shakespeare and the Globe by Aliki (HarperCollins, 1999): This well-researched look at Shakespeare's life includes the reconstruction of the Globe Theatre.

Web Sites

Mr. William Shakespeare and the Internet

shakespeare.palomar.edu/intro.htm

An interactive time line and biographical chart tell the story of Shakespeare's life.

National Geographic for Kids

www.nationalgeographic.com/kids

View video, hear audio, and see a map showing where gorillas live.

Plimoth Plantation

www.plimoth.org

Take a virtual tour of Plimoth Plantation.

Savage Seas

www.pbs.org/wnet/savageseas

Use a wave simulator and explore tsunamis, freak waves, and trade winds.

Magic Tree House
Passport

Name: _____

```
Paste a picture
of yourself here.
```

Title: _____
_____

Time: _____

Place: _____

①

Magic Book:

_____
_____

Mission:

_____
_____
_____
_____

Danger:

_____
_____
_____
_____

②

Itinerary

Event 1: _____

Event 2: _____

Event 3: _____

Event 4: _____

Event 5: _____

Other Important Events:

_____
_____
_____
_____

③

Who Jack and Annie Meet:

_____
_____
_____
_____
_____

What Jack and Annie Learn:

_____
_____
_____
_____

④

Words to Know

Magic Tree House Title: _____

Word	I know what it means!	I can say it, but I'm not sure what it means.	I've never seen this word before!

Teaching With Favorite Magic Tree House Books   Scholastic Teaching Resources

- ◎ **Dinosaurs Before Dark**
  (Random House, 1992)

- ◎ **The Knight at Dawn**
  (Random House, 1993)

- ◎ **Mummies in the Morning**
  (Random House, 1993)

- ◎ **Pirates Past Noon**
  (Random House, 1994)

In the first four Magic Tree House books, Mary Pope Osborne introduces readers to a brother and sister. Careful and scholarly Jack and courageous and spontaneous Annie find a tree house in the woods behind their home in Frog Creek, Pennsylvania. They soon discover that it is a magic tree house that contains books that can transport them to different places and time periods.

Catching the Clues

Jack and Annie have a mystery to solve. Who is the owner of the tree house? Each book in this cluster contains one clue to help them figure it out. In *Dinosaurs Before Dark*, the clue is a gold medallion with the letter *M* on it. In *The Knight at Dawn*, it's a fancy bookmark with an *M* on it. After returning from ancient Egypt in *Mummies in the Morning*, they see a shimmering *M* on the tree house floor. Finally, they solve the mystery when the parrot they met in *Pirates Past Noon* turns into the mysterious *M* person—an enchanted librarian named Morgan le Fay.

Fact Finders Scavenger Hunt

Take children's interests in the science and history behind this cluster further with this scavenger hunt. To set up the scavenger hunt, copy the questions below on the chalkboard or make photocopies for children. Use the questions as a springboard for further investigation. If a research guide is available, have students use the index to look up additional information on each answer.

1. What kind of dinosaur do Jack and Annie meet that has a mouth like a pair of scissors, feels fuzzy, and has a crest on its head? (*pteranodon*)

2. Why aren't Jack and Annie afraid to approach the triceratops eating flowers? (*He is a plant eater, not a meat eater!*)

3. If you were invited to a feast in a medieval castle, what could you expect to find on the menu? (*whole pigs, pies, and peacocks with all their feathers*)

4. When wrapping a mummy, ancient Egyptians used something you might find on your kitchen table. What is it? (*salt*)

5. Jack and Annie see an Egyptian funeral procession in the desert. Annie thinks it is a ghostly parade, but Jack says it is just one of those scientific occurrences. What is the word for what he is describing? (*a mirage*)

Dinosaurs Before Dark

Before You Read

In *Dinosaurs Before Dark* Jack and Annie are whisked back to prehistoric times where they encounter dinosaurs galore. Have students look closely at the cover of the book and describe what they see. Invite them to make a triple prediction about Annie, Jack, and the dinosaur: What role will each play in this adventure?

After You Read

Make Jack Guess
(Science and Language Arts)

Jack fills his notebook with facts about dinosaurs. Let students take turns playing Jack to test their dinosaur knowledge. Have each student choose a dinosaur. Ask children to record facts about their dinosaur, such as size, features, food, and time period. (The research guide is a good resource.) Invite a child to play the role of Jack. Ask a volunteer to reveal facts about his or her dinosaur without sharing its identity. If Jack guesses the dinosaur correctly, he or she stays in the chair. If Jack's guess is incorrect, the other student takes the chair. The game continues until all students have shared their research.

Digging for Dinosaurs
(Science)

Explain that scientists who study prehistoric life are called paleontologists. Let students practice paleontologist skills with this puzzling activity:

- Enlarge the dinosaurs on page 21. Make several copies of each and laminate for durability. Cut each dinosaur into puzzle pieces. Place each set of pieces in a numbered envelope.
- Divide the class into teams. Have each team put a puzzle together and record the following information: Envelope Number, Number of Pieces, Characteristics, Dinosaur's Identity, Deciding Reasons for This Identification. Encourage students to use the research guide to assist in identifying the dinosaurs.
- Rotate the envelopes so that each team gets a chance to solve several puzzles. Bring students together to discuss findings. Did students agree on the identifications? If not, what might have been confusing?

Counting Baby Dinosaurs (Math)

Jack and Annie stumble upon Anatosaurus nests filled with eggs—a perfect invitation for practicing multiplication.

- Divide the class into small groups. Give each group ten small paper cups (nests) and a handful of dried beans (dinosaur eggs).
- Write a multiplication problem on the chalkboard—for example, 3 x 7. Explain that the first number is the number of nests (3) and the second is the number of eggs per nest (7).
- Let students use their nests and eggs to show the problem and find the solution. Repeat with new problems.
- Follow up by letting children write word problems to share—for example, "Jack and Annie found 6 Anatosaurus nests with 5 eggs each. They found 4 Stegosaurus nests with 4 eggs each. How many eggs did they find all together?"

Dinosaurs

by Will Osborne and Mary Pope Osborne
(Random House, 2002)

Students can use this research guide to discover how dinosaurs got their names. List several dinosaurs included in the guide, such as Iguanodon, Megalosaurus, Alamosaurus, Corythosaurus, and Oviraptor. Have students record the names and tell how they think each got its name. Students can check their guesses with the research guide, using the index to find what they're looking for fast!

Paleontologist's Puzzle

① **Apatosaurus**

② **Triceratops**

③ **Stegosaurus**

④ **Tyrannosaurus**

Teaching With Favorite Magic Tree House Books
Scholastic Teaching Resources

The Knight at Dawn

Before You Read

Jack and Annie find themselves in the Middle Ages at a feast where they are not welcome. Ask students to think about their own lives: What kinds of foods do they eat? What clothes do they wear? What kind of home do they live in? As they read this story, encourage children to compare modern times to the Middle Ages.

After You Read

Knights Weigh In (Math)

Jack has trouble trying on a knight's helmet. He reads that it is heavy, sometimes weighing up to forty pounds, and compares wearing a helmet to having a five-year-old on his head! Let students make their own weight comparisons to learn more. On the chalkboard, list the weight of various parts of a knight's armor:

Mail shirt: 25 pounds
Full suit of armor: 65 pounds
Tournament armor: 120 pounds
Helmet: 40 pounds
Sword: 3 pounds
Shield: 10 pounds

Have students use a scale to find something that weighs as much as each of the items listed. Discuss how wearing armor might make simple tasks, such as getting up and down stairs, difficult.

Castle Parts and Purposes

(Art and Language Arts)

As he and Annie explore medieval times, Jack records information in his notebook about the parts of a castle—for example, drawbridge, moat, and hawk house—each of which serves an important purpose. Share the diagram in the *Knights and Castles Research Guide* (pages 38–39). Invite students to use the research guide as a model to design, diagram, and label their own castle. What do the castles have in common? How are they different?

Get Out of the Dungeon!

(Language Arts and Math)

Jack and Annie use a map of the castle to escape from the dungeon. Students can use what they learn in the book to escape from a dungeon, too. Give each child a copy of page 23. Have students read and answer the True or False questions in turn to find their way out of the castle. Each question tests their comprehension skills and each answer takes them a different way. This self-checking maze may inspire students to create their own. Photocopy the mazes they make for classmates to try!

Magic Tree House **Research Guide**

Knights

by Will Osborne and Mary Pope Osborne
(Random House, 2000)

Nonfiction books sometimes use a pattern of organization that describes or lists information. In this research guide, students can recognize that structure in the descriptions of the castles, castle life, and so on. Set up a chart to learn more. Use chapter titles for headings. Read aloud a detail from one of those chapters. Have students tell which section of the chart it goes with and record it. Continue, until students have identified several details for each section of the chart. Have students use the details to summarize the main, or most important, idea of each set of details.

Name _____ Date _____

Get Out of the Dungeon!

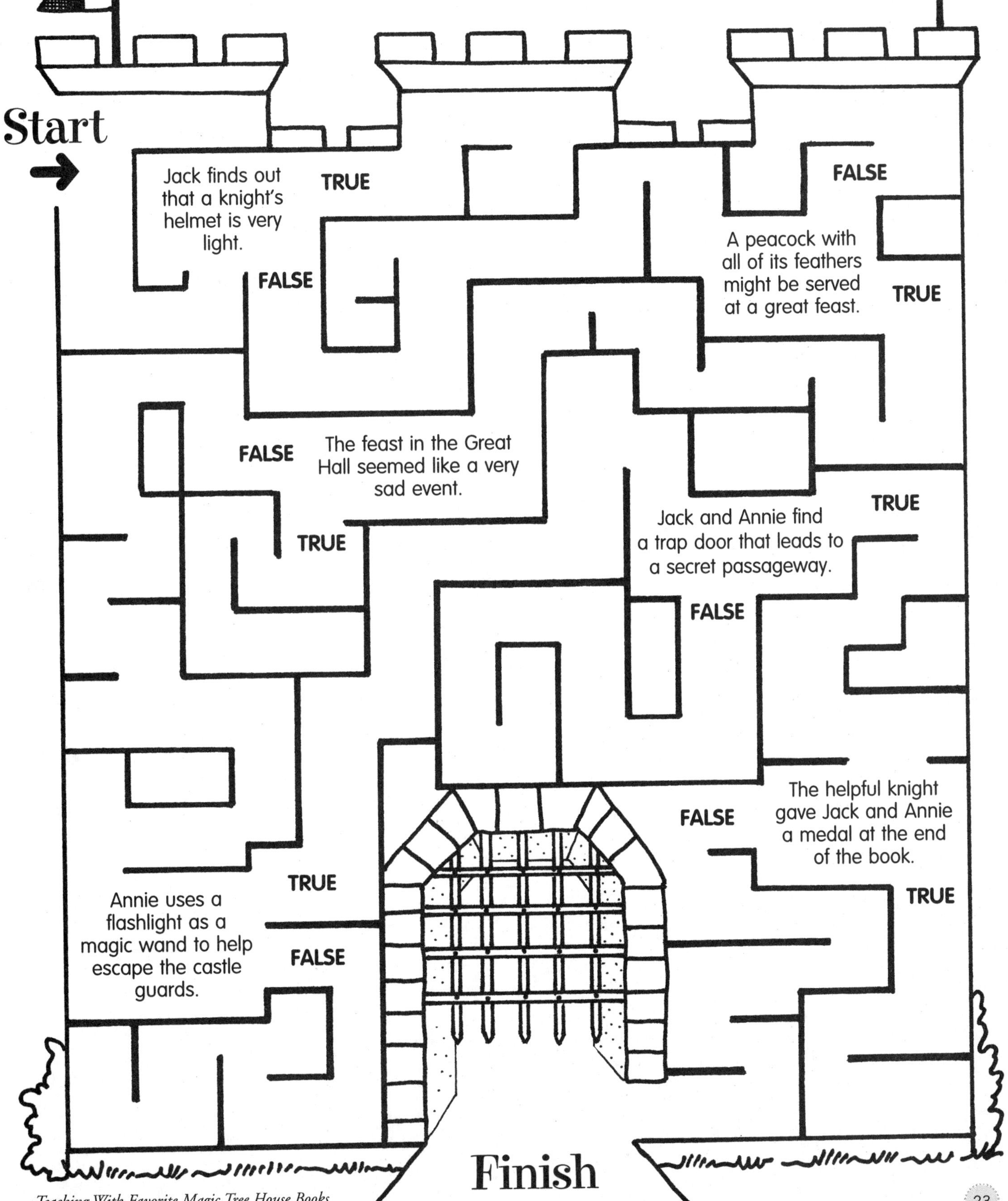

Start →

Jack finds out that a knight's helmet is very light.

TRUE

FALSE

FALSE

A peacock with all of its feathers might be served at a great feast.

TRUE

FALSE

The feast in the Great Hall seemed like a very sad event.

TRUE

Jack and Annie find a trap door that leads to a secret passageway.

TRUE

FALSE

The helpful knight gave Jack and Annie a medal at the end of the book.

FALSE

TRUE

Annie uses a flashlight as a magic wand to help escape the castle guards.

TRUE

FALSE

Finish

Mummies in the Morning

Jack and Annie travel to ancient Egypt, where they meet the ghost of an Egyptian queen. Share pictures of pyramids with students. Explain that Jack and Annie explore the inside of a pyramid. Ask students to predict what Jack and Annie will find. Record their predictions. Let students revise their ideas after reading to reflect what they've learned.

After You Read

See, Define, Draw
(Language Arts, Social Studies, and Art)

This book takes students far back in time and introduces them to content-area vocabulary accordingly. To build independence in learning new words, try a multisensory approach. Give each child a copy of page 25. (Add new words before copying if desired.) For "See," have students copy the word and highlight memorable features, such as the double -m in mummy. For "Define," have them tell what the word means. For "Draw," have them draw a picture that illustrates the meaning. (Adapted from Stretching Students' Vocabulary by Karen Bromley; Scholastic, 2002.)

It's a Wrap!
(Dramatic Play and Math)

As they explore the inside of the pyramid, Jack and Annie discover a mummy and Jack reads about mummification in his book. Bodies were wrapped tightly from head to toe in linen strips soaked in resin (a hardening agent). The whole process took about 15 days, using 1,000 yards of 2- to 8-inch-wide linen. Have students see how long it would take them to wrap a mummy. Divide the class into groups. Give each group a roll of toilet tissue. Have one person in each group be the mummy. Teammates work together to wrap the mummy from toes to neck (leaving the head uncovered for safety) in the least amount of time.

Building a Mystery
(Language Arts)

How do authors hold their readers' interest from beginning to end? One way is by building suspense. In adventure books, it seems that just as the characters have gotten out of one dilemma, they are involved in another. These challenges make them work even harder, and keeps readers cheering for them. Invite children to identify the challenges in Mummies in the Morning. For example, when Jack and Annie follow the cat into the pyramid, they think they see a tomb robber. As soon as they figure out it's not a tomb robber, they find out it's a ghost! Have students do the same with other books in the series. Discuss plot patterns that emerge. Have students imagine other obstacles Jack and Annie could have encountered in ancient Egypt and write a new story!

Mummies and Pyramids
by Will Osborne and Mary Pope Osborne
(Random House, 2001)

Use this guide to play a game of What's the Question. To play, find and state the answer to a question—for example, "The Nile." Have children use the research guide to find out what the question is, write it on a slip of paper, ("What's the name of the river that flows through Egypt?"), and place it in a box. Reveal the question at the end of the day, and post a new answer for the next day. Review use of an index and skimming skills to prepare for this activity. (Use children's answers to guide instruction in using the Research Guides.)

See, Define, Draw

Word	👁 See	☁ Define	✏ Draw
pyramid			
sarcophagus			
mummy			
scepter			
tomb			
hieroglyph			

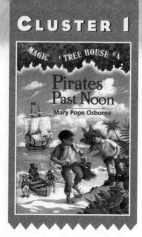

Pirates Past Noon

In *Pirates Past Noon* Jack and Annie have to survive the days of deserted islands and plundering pirates. Make a list of pirate words students know—for example, *aye*, *lubber*, *hoist*, *mutineers*, and *plank*. Work together to define the words. After reading the book, students can add to the list to see how their vocabulary from this time in history has grown!

After You Read

Hidden Treasures
(Language Arts)

Cap'n Bones was searching for buried treasure. Jack and Annie help him find the booty by reading a map and solving a riddle. Invite students to practice similar skills.

- Have each child bring in a small wrapped trinket from home (with permission).
- Let children hide their trinkets in the classroom. Have children write riddles that will lead to their "buried treasure."
- Roll up the riddles like parchment and distribute randomly to children. Let students solve the riddle to find the prize.

Pirate Ship Coordinates (Math)

This twist on Battleship incorporates the use of the Cartesian coordinate system and makes learning about coordinates fun and unforgettable. Give children a copy of page 27. Have them cut out the ships and tape them to the grid (lining them up with the squares). Pair up students and have them sit back-to-back. Let them take turns calling out coordinates to locate each other's ships. They can mark successful guesses in one color and unsuccessful ones in another (or just record them on a separate sheet of paper).

Treasure Chest (Math)

In the days of pirates, treasure chests could contain all sorts of valuable objects. Reinforce math skills with this treasure chest center.

- Decorate a small shoe box as a treasure chest. Stock it with trinkets (play coins, rings, necklaces, crowns, and so on). On the inside of the lid, make a key that shows what different treasures are worth—for example, ring: 25 cents.
- Invite students to scoop out some treasure and count up their booty. (The word booty refers to anything valuable that is taken from another ship or person, such as money and jewels.)
- Students can compare how much of each part of the treasure they find (3 rings, 5 coins, 2 necklaces), what the total value of each kind of treasure is, and what the overall value is.

Pirates

by Will Osborne and Mary Pope Osborne
(Random House, 2001)

Extend learning with a trivia game. Let students use the research guide to find facts about pirates. Have them write a set of three or four related questions that increase in difficulty on one side of an index card. They can color code the questions by difficulty level (for example, easy: yellow; medium: green; difficult: blue), and write the answers on the back. Students can use the cards to quiz each other and learn more!

Pirate Ship Coordinates

10
9
8
7
6
5
4
3
2
1

A B C D E F G H I J

Jack and Annie travel through time, from ancient Japan where they meet ninjas and samurais to a futuristic space port on the moon. Along the way they meet prehistoric creatures such as the woolly mammoth and discover rain forest animals in the Amazon.

As the first book, *Night of the Ninjas*, opens, Jack and Annie find a mysterious note from Morgan le Fay. It says, "Help me—Under a spell—Find 4 things." At the end of this book, they are given the first thing— a moonstone from a Ninja master. In *Afternoon on the Amazon*, a monkey gives them a mango. A mammoth bone from *Sunset of the Sabertooth* and a mouse from *Midnight on the Moon* help the brother and sister complete their mission.

Fact Finders Scavenger Hunt

Challenge children to uncover facts about prehistoric times, the Amazon, space, and more with this scavenger hunt. To set up the scavenger hunt, copy the questions below on the chalkboard or make photocopies for children. Use the answers as a springboard for further investigation. If a research guide is available, have students use the index to look up additional information on each answer.

1. In *Night of the Ninjas*, Jack writes in his notebook: "1. use nature 2. be nature 3. follow nature." Find an example of each in the book. (*use nature: Jack and Annie use sticks to make a moon dial; be nature: They pretend to be a rock; follow nature: They follow the mouse out of the icy water.*)

2. What is it about the Amazon's army ants that send animals and Jack and Annie fleeing in panic? (*they're flesh-eating creatures and march through the forest by the millions*)

3. Pretend you are living in the Cro-Magnon age. How would you make a coat, a lamp, and a musical instrument? (*coat: scrape reindeer skin with rocks and use a bone needle to sew skins together; lamp: hollow out a rock, fill it with animal fat and use moss to make a wick; musical instrument: make a flute out of mammoth bones*)

4. Jack and Annie find astronaut footprints from many years ago. Why are they still there? (*There is no rain or wind on the moon to wash or blow them away!*)

5. If the moon's temperature reaches 260° Fahrenheit, how do moon scientists protect themselves? (*by wearing spacesuits with controls to keep them from getting too hot*)

Night of the Ninjas

Before You Read

Jack and Annie travel back in time to the secret cave of a Ninja master in ancient Japan. Locate Japan on a world map. Discuss where Japan is in relation to where students live.

After You Read

Map Making
(Social Studies and Art)

When Jack and Annie travel back to ancient Japan, they observe the topography of the region. Provide practice with using nonfiction graphic aids by letting students translate details about Japan's topography to a map. As a class, list geographic landforms mentioned in the book, such as mountains, rivers, caves, and trees. Give students a sheet of drawing paper. Have them draw a horizontal line across the bottom of the page about two inches from the bottom. This will be the map's legend. Ask students to draw symbols in the legend to represent the various land formations. Then have them use these symbols to draw a map of ancient Japan through Jack's eyes.

Shadows and Sundials
(Science and Math)

Jack and Annie use the shadow of the sun to help them travel back to the tree house. A sundial is the oldest known device for showing the time of day. It measures the angle of a shadow cast by the sun on a pointer. Here's a simple sundial to make.

- Label the sides of a cardboard square (approximately 14 inches) "North," "South," "East," and "West."

- Mark the center point of the square. Glue a paper towel tube at the mark so it stands perpendicular to the cardboard. Let dry overnight.

- Take the sundial outside. Position the north end on the ground facing north. At the top of each hour, mark where the tube casts a shadow, and label the time.

Move Like a Ninja
(Movement and History)

Jack reads in his book that Ninjas fought to protect their families. Ninjas perfected a system of martial arts called Ninjutsu. In Ninjutsu, kamae are the starting positions from which all the other techniques are created. Have students practice some Ninja positions:

- **Fudoza no kamae (immovable seat):** This sitting position allowed Samurai to stand quickly and draw their swords. To do this, sit on the floor with your right leg tucked under your bottom. Position the left leg straight out in front and then pull it in so that the inside of the left foot touches the inside of the right leg.

- **Hira no kamae (one-line receiving posture):** This standing position is effective in giving the opponent the impression that you are vulnerable to attack. To try this, spread legs a little further than shoulder width. Lift and spread arms out to each side with fingers straight but touching each other; wrists are straight.

Afternoon on the Amazon

Before You Read

Jack and Annie are off to a rain forest full of exotic animals. Help students locate the Amazon on a map and share what they know about rain forests. What animals would they expect to see? What climate would they find? Encourage children to be alert for new information as they read.

After You Read

Three-Layer Mural
(Science and Art)

Tropical rain forests have three layers: the canopy (top), the understory (middle) and the forest floor (bottom). Explore life in each layer with a collaborative mural.

● Divide the class into three groups. Assign each group a layer. Using *Magic Tree House Research Guide: Rain Forests*, invite children to list what they'd find in each layer. For example, tree trunks, rotting leaves, and bushes inhabited by jaguars, snakes, and insects are part of the forest floor.

● Give each group a sheet of mural paper. Have students illustrate their group's layer and use labels and captions to add information. Arrange the mural sections in order on a wall.

Setting the Scene
(Language Arts)

"Jack felt something cold and scaly as he touched the snake." Mary Pope Osborne uses Jack and Annie's senses to bring the rain forest to life. To explore this technique, divide the class into groups. Give each group a copy of the graphic organizer on page 31. Using multiple copies of the book, have students locate and record descriptions that appeal to each sense. Bring the class together to share findings. How many different examples did students find? Have students choose a setting for a new Magic Tree House book and write a description of this setting that draws on each of the senses.

Rain Forests All Around (Science)

Learn more about what Jack and Annie discover in the rain forest by sharing this scenario:

You wake up and have cereal and a banana for breakfast, and then get on the bus to go to school. At school you sit at your wooden desk and look forward to the chocolate treat in your lunch box.

Ask students how many items in the description are from the rain forest. (*banana, rubber wheels on the bus, wood for desk and chair, chocolate from the cacao bean*) Learn about other items that come from rain forests, such as coffee, medicine, spices, and chicle (the ingredient that makes gum chewy). Challenge students to be rain forest detectives in their homes. Have them document what they find, telling the place (such as the kitchen cupboard) and the product.

Rain Forests
by Will Osborne and Mary Pope Osborne
(Random House, 2001)

Challenge students to take what they learn in this research guide further by creating an A to Z rain forest encyclopedia. Have students work together to find and illustrate interesting facts for each letter of the alphabet. (Guide students to recognize the usefulness of the index for this.) Combine children's research in a binder to create an inventive classroom resource.

Name _____

Date _____

Setting the Scene

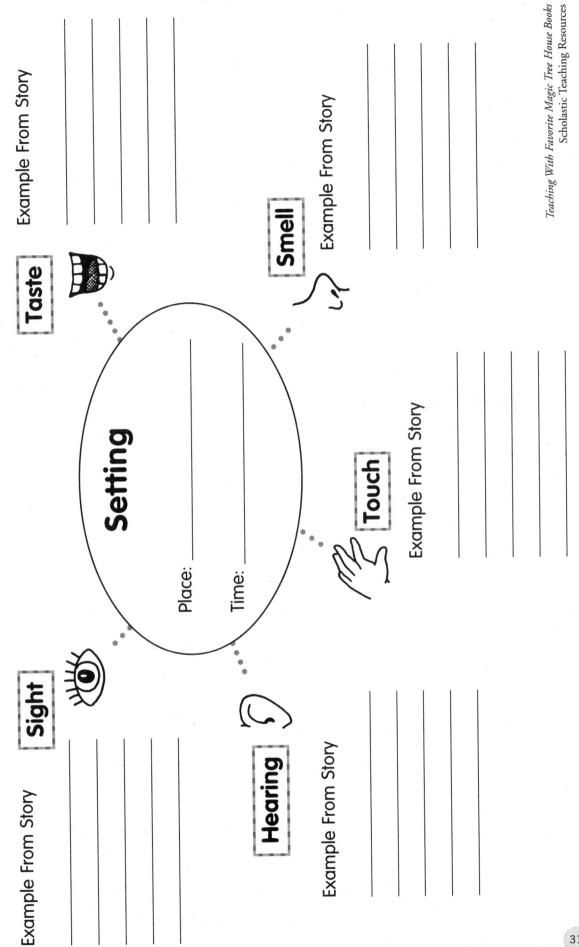

Sight

Example From Story
_____
_____
_____
_____

Taste

Example From Story
_____
_____
_____
_____

Smell

Example From Story
_____
_____
_____
_____

Setting

Place: _____

Time: _____

Touch

Example From Story
_____
_____
_____
_____

Hearing

Example From Story
_____
_____
_____
_____

Teaching With Favorite Magic Tree House Books
Scholastic Teaching Resources

Sunset of the Sabertooth

Before You Read

Jack and Annie are whisked back to the Ice Age. They learn about cave people and how they survived the elements. Jack and Annie have to learn something about woolly mammoths and sabertoothed tigers to survive, too. Before reading the book, discuss how animals protect themselves from the cold. What do people use? Invite students to pretend they are going back in time to the Ice Age. What supplies would they bring?

After You Read

Picture This (Language Arts, Art, and Social Studies)

The ability to read an author's words and visualize what he or she is writing about is a skill readers need to practice. Although Magic Tree House books do have some illustrations that support the text, because they are chapter books, not all ideas are represented with pictures. With *Sunset of the Sabertooth*, students will notice that Jack often refers to pictures in the book he is reading (*Life in the Ice Age*) as he shares the captions with Annie. Read these passages aloud, encouraging students to use the details they hear to make pictures in their minds. Then have them draw what they imagine the pictures in Jack's book look like. Have students write new captions to go with their pictures. Follow up by looking at pictures and diagrams in various Magic Tree House research guides. Guide children to understand how they can use this feature of nonfiction books to get information, just like Jack!

Cave Art
(Social Studies and Art)

Jack and Annie discover the beautiful cave paintings of the Cro-Magnon after crawling through a tunnel in a cave. They see pictures of bison, mammoths, bears, and reindeer. Annie compares it to an art gallery. Invite students to create an Ice Age gallery of their own by constructing a cave mural in the classroom. Cover a wall in the classroom with craft paper. Let students sketch ideas for the classroom "cave," using events in their own lives as inspiration. Have them transfer their ideas to the mural paper, using red and black paints (the colors used in Cro-Magnon cave drawings). If someone were to discover these cave paintings thousands of years from now, what would they say about life today?

Ice Age Pet Shop
(Science and Language Arts)

In *Sunset of the Sabertooth*, Jack and Annie are introduced to many of the animals that lived during the Ice Age. Invite students to name various animals mentioned in the book— including sabertoothed tiger, woolly mammoth, reindeer, bison, woolly rhino, lion, bear, and elk. Have each student choose an animal to research. Create an Ice Age Pet Shop as a way for students to share their findings. Students can draw a picture of the animal on a sheet of paper and write information about it on an index card. Combine pictures and index cards in a display.

Midnight on the Moon

Jack and Annie travel to the future (for the first time) and land on the moon! Invite students to predict some of the difficulties they might encounter on the moon. Discuss what life might be like in the year 2031.

Create a Crater (Science)

Craters make for a very bumpy ride on the moon buggy. How were those craters created? Billions of years ago giant-sized asteroids hit the moon's surface. The same thing happened to Earth, but over time wind, rain, and water eroded the craters. Craters on the moon exist because there is no wind or water. Explore crater formation with this demonstration.

● Cover the floor with newspaper. Place a cake pan on the newspaper. Fill the pan with flour and smooth out the surface.

● Coat the flour with a sprinkling of powdered chocolate. (The contrast in color will help children observe crater formations.)

● Hold a small object (such as a marble) a few feet above the pan. Count along with children to three, then drop it. Repeat with other objects (such as golf balls and small stones) to form different-sized craters.

● Discuss what caused the different sizes and shapes. (*weight and size of object, height from which it's dropped*)

Day on the Moon
(Science and Movement)

Send students on their own moon mission with these activities:

Moon Walk: Provide a pair of large sponges and two extra large rubber bands. Invite students to take turns fastening the sponges to their feet with the rubber bands and taking a short walk around the classroom. This activity gives them the feel of what it could be like to walk on the moon.

We Were Here! Jack and Annie find the flag that astronauts planted in 1969. It remains standing because there is no wind or rain to knock it over. Jack and Annie think carefully about what they want their message on the moon to say. Have kids create their own moon message flags and a "moon" on which to display them.

Space
by Will Osborne and Mary Pope Osborne
(Random House, 2002)

This guide expands on Annie and Jack's space exploration with information about Galileo, Sir Isaac Newton, John Glenn, Neil Armstrong, Sally Ride, Mae Jemison, and other history makers. Use the guide as a springboard for publishing a class collection of biographies about space explorers. Share picture book biographies (see Resources, pages 15–16) as models. Guide children to recognize a common structure of biographies— sequence or time order. Notice words that signal order, such as *first, second, before, after, at the same time, finally,* and *following.* Students can use time lines, fun facts, and other features of nonfiction books to bring their biographies to life.

◎ **Dolphins at Daybreak** (Random House, 1997)

◎ **Ghost Town at Sundown** (Random House, 1998)

◎ **Lions at Lunchtime** (Random House, 1998)

◎ **Polar Bears Past Bedtime** (Random House, 1998)

This group of books takes Jack and Annie from the depths of a coral reef to a spooky ghost town in the Old West, from the warmth of the African savanna to the frigid temperatures of the Arctic. They learn about dolphins, mustangs, lions, and polar bears along the way.

Catching the Clues

In this cluster, Jack and Annie need to solve four riddles in order to become master librarians. Being master librarians will allow them to gather books for Morgan le Fay's library. Along the way, they travel to a coral reef, where they find the answer to the first riddle—an oyster. Next, they travel to the Old West and figure out that the answer to the next riddle is an echo. Honey is the answer to the riddle in *Lions at Lunchtime*. They find the answer to the last riddle in a mask that a seal hunter gives them in *Polar Bears Past Bedtime*. When they put the first letters from those four objects together they form a word: *home*. This is the place they love best, and also where Morgan rewards both Jack and Annie with their master librarian cards.

Fact Finders Scavenger Hunt

Guide children to pay attention to particulars about the creatures Jack and Annie encounter in their travels with this scavenger hunt. To set up the scavenger hunt, copy the questions below on the chalkboard or make photocopies for children. Use the answers as a springboard for further investigation. If a research guide is available, have students use the index to look up additional information on each answer.

(1) Jack and Annie discover that the coral reef is home to more than 5,000 kinds of creatures. Name three. (*starfish, jellyfish, sea horses, giant clam, stingray, dolphin, octopus, and so on*)

(2) What safety tip do Jack and Annie follow when they encounter a shark? (*they don't splash; they swim calmly away*)

(3) What rules do Jack and Annie discover are helpful in caring for a wild horse? (*soft hand, firm voice, sunny disposition, praise and rewards*)

(4) What household item is about as big as a giraffe's hoof? (*a dinner plate*)

(5) If ice is too thin to hold the weight of a person, how could a polar bear weighing 750 pounds walk on it without falling through? (*by distributing its weight and sliding its paws*)

Dolphins at Daybreak

Before You Read

Jack and Annie explore the ocean in a submarine. Make a list of creatures students think Jack and Annie might see. As students read the book, have them check off any that are mentioned in the book.

After You Read

Make a Submersible

(Science)

Jack and Annie go for a thrilling ride in a submarine. Use this demonstration to explore how a submarine works.

- To make a submarine, stick a small piece of clay to the bottom of the clip on a pen cap. Place the pen cap clip-end down in a container of water. Add or remove clay until only the tip of the cap is visible above the water.

- Fill a plastic liter bottle with water. Place the submarine inside and secure the lid. Squeeze the sides of the bottle. What happens? (*Water is forced into the pen cap. This displaces air and makes the cap heavier, which causes it to sink.*)

- Release the sides of the bottle. What happens? (*Water moves out of the pen cap and makes it lighter, which allows it to float.*)

- Based on their observations, how do students think a submarine works? (*To dive, the submarine has tanks that are flooded with water. To surface, air is pumped into the tanks, driving out the water and making it float.*)

Ship's Log

(Language Arts and Science)

When Annie asks Jack what a ship's log is, he explains that it is a diary of an ocean trip. Have students keep their own ship's log to practice summarizing skills. Review what a summay is by having students describe their day in detail. Next have them summarize, including just the important details. Discuss how summarizing helps readers remember what's important. Model writing a chapter summary. Then have students try. How few words can they use to capture what's really important? As a variation, have students keep a log that summarizes factual information from each chapter on the left page, and fiction on the right.

Classroom Aquarium

(Art and Science)

Create a classroom aquarium to show what Jack and Annie observe as they travel along the coral reef. Have students research several facts about a sea creature from the book and record the information on an index card. Give each child two paper plates. Have children cut out the center of one paper plate and cover the hole with blue cellophane. Have children draw a picture of the sea creature in the center area of the second paper plate, adding details such as sand, coral, and seaweed. Help children place the plates together, insides facing each other, and staple around the rim. Display the aquarium windows with captions.

Magic Tree House **Research Guide**

Dolphins and Sharks
by Mary Pope Osborne and Natalie Pope Boyce
(Random House, 2003)

How much do students know about dolphins and sharks? Find out with a sorting game. Use the research guide to gather facts specific to dolphins and sharks. Write the facts on index cards (one per card) but do not reveal whether they pertain to dolphins or sharks (for example, "can dive up to 1,000 feet"). Have students use the research guide to determine whether each fact is about dolphins or sharks and sort the cards accordingly.

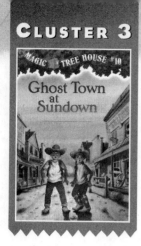

Ghost Town at Sundown

Jack and Annie find themselves in a Wild West adventure as they help to rescue a stolen mustang. Along the way, they learn about a mysterious ghost town from a cowboy named Slim. Ask students to predict what they think a ghost town is. Invite them to look at the picture on the cover and use the words *ghost* and *town* to come up with a definition.

After You Read

All About the Old West

(Math and History)

What are wild horses called? Is a mustang's family important? The answers to these questions and more are part of Jack and Annie's story. To help students become familiar with nonfiction writing, let them combine facts from the story about the Old West. They might be surprised to learn that their nonfiction doesn't have to be a paragraph. It can be a diagram, map, chart, pamphlet, letter (or e-mail), or newspaper article! Use a research guide to share examples of nonfiction in different forms. Then challenge students to organize their facts in any way *but* a paragraph. For example, they might make a chart to compare life in the Old West with life today, write a glossary, create an illustration with captions, or use a word web to present key vocabulary. Display students' work and notice the many ways they found to share the same information.

Five Simple Rules

(Language Arts and Math)

Jack learns a few simple rules for how to treat a horse: soft hand, firm voice, sunny attitude, praise, and reward. These rules, or how-to's, come in handy when Jack has to keep Dusty quiet. Ask children how rules and how-to directions are handy in everyday life. (*For example, people follow how-to directions to put things together; students follow how-to rules for getting along in the classroom.*) Let children practice this nonfiction writing skill by making a set of how-to rules or directions for something they do well—for example, "how to shoot a basket" or "how to keep your cubby neat." Discuss this kind of writing with other forms, such as letters or reports.

Echo Makers (Science)

Jack and Annie must solve this riddle: "Out of the blue, my lonely voice calls out to you. Who am I? Who Am I?" Later in the story, the kids camp out in Blue Canyon, where they discover the answer to the riddle. (*an echo*) Investigate the science behind echoes with this demonstration.

- Find a brick wall outside of the school. Clap two pieces of wood together near the wall. What do students hear? (*When you are close to the wall, the sound travels so quickly that the original sound and the reflected sound seem like one.*)

- Slowly back away from the wall while clapping the wood. What do students hear? (*They will hear the sound as it goes out away from the blocks. They will hear the sound again—the echo—as it is reflected back from the wall.*)

Lions at Lunchtime

Before You Read

Jack and Annie travel to the African Plains, where they witness the migration of wild animals across a river. After following a special bird, they are able to give an unusual gift to a Masai warrior. Before reading the book, ask students to imagine the African plains. What animals would they see? What is the landscape like? As children read, they can compare their ideas with what they learn about the setting.

After You Read

Take Note
(Language Arts and Science)

Wherever the Magic Tree House takes Jack and Annie, Jack records facts in his notebook. Revisit Jack's notes. What do they have in common? (*He doesn't use complete sentences. He jots down key words, such as, "animals all connected."*) Explore the difference between taking notes and writing sentences. Write Jack's notes on the chalkboard. Have children take turns using them to write complete sentences. Explain that note-taking is a quick way to record information. Notes are turned into sentences when it's time to write the first draft of a report or presentation. For practice, have students research an African plains animal (giraffe, elephant, zebra, wildebeest, gazelle, lion, vulture, hyena, honey guide bird). Challenge students to write five facts using only three or four words per fact.

African Index
(Language Arts and Study Skills)

"Sensing that the lions are not hunting at the moment, the other animals graze nearby." Jack and Annie learn this and so much more as they travel the expansive African plains. Since there are numerous nonfiction topics presented, invite students to make an index for the book, so that "researchers" can easily find information they're looking for. Let students begin by recording topics on index cards (one per card). Have them arrange the cards (topics) in alphabetical order. Students can then copy the alphabetized topics on chart paper (for an easy-to-read reference), and add page numbers where the information is located. Sample index entries include:

giraffe, 15–16
hyena, 28–29
migration, 10–11
zebra, 10, 16–17

Roar Like a Lion
(Language Arts and Writing)

In *Lions at Lunchtime*, Mary Pope Osborne takes readers to the wild plains of Africa where they learn about some amazing African animals. In order to make her writing more descriptive, the author uses similes and metaphors. This writer's tool compares one object to another in order to paint a vivid picture. Similes use the words *like* or *as*—for example, "The giraffe's hooves are as big as dinner plates." Metaphors make comparisons without the words *like* or *as*—for example, "The elephant's spray was a strong shower." Challenge students to find more similes and metaphors in the book. Then have students come up with their own comparisons to use in their writing. Students' writing will be as colorful as a rainbow!

Polar Bears Past Bedtime

Before You Read

Jack and Annie travel to the Arctic region, where they get stuck on cracking ice. Let students locate this region on a globe. Discuss weather conditions here. Brainstorm what someone traveling to this area would need to pack—for example, warm parka, boots, and a dogsled.

After You Read

Astonishing Animals
(Language Arts and Science)

In the foreword to this book, Mary Pope Osborne explains that one astonishing fact inspired her to write this story: Polar bears can walk on ice even though they weigh as much as 1,000 pounds! Invite students to research an animal, looking for one astonishing fact. Have students create an "Astonishing Animal Fact Card" with the information. On one side of an oaktag card, have them draw and label the animal. On the reverse, have them record the astonishing fact. Students can trade their cards to learn about these astonishing animals! Encourage students to use their facts as inspiration for stories they write.

Keeping Warm (Science)

As Jack and Annie discover, the Arctic is a very cold place! The temperature outside can drop to -37° Celsius. A seal hunter gives them a parka made of sealskin, but how do Arctic animals keep warm? Seals, walruses, and polar bears have a layer of fat (up to 4 inches thick!) called blubber.

Explore the science behind this with a simple experiment.

- Place a scoop of vegetable shortening in a container. Fill two glasses with ice water.

- Have students thoroughly coat one of their index fingers with a layer of shortening. Invite each student to dip the shortening-coated finger in one glass and a bare finger in the other. Compare results. Which finger got cold first? (For easy cleanup, students can place their hand in a sandwich bag before coating a finger with the shortening. In this case, they should also place the hand without the shortening in a sandwich bag.)

Paw Print Diagrams
(Science)

A seal hunter explains that polar bears have taught his people many things about living in the Arctic. A polar bear's body has lots of adaptations, including its paws, for surviving the harsh environment. Students can explore this by making and labeling paw print diagrams. For each student provide a ruler, white construction paper, black

sandpaper, paper clips, plastic wrap, and cotton balls.

- Draw a 12-inch line across the center of the construction paper. This is about how wide a polar bear paw is. Use the line as a guide to draw a 12-inch circle (the paw print).

- Cut out five circular pieces of sandpaper to make toes and one large circle for the heel. Attach a paper clip "claw" to each toe and glue the toes to the paw print, rough side up. Leave space between each toe. Glue the heel, rough side up, to the other end of the paw.

- Glue a piece of plastic wrap (webbing) in the shape of a half circle between each toe. Fill the remaining area of the paw with cotton balls (fur) and glue in place.

- Glue the paw to a large sheet of paper. Use call-outs (captions with arrows pointing to the corresponding area of the paw) to explain the functions of each paw part—for example, "A rough pad provides traction on ice and snow. Fur protects the paws from the cold. Webbing between the toes helps with swimming."

- ◎ **Vacation Under the Volcano**
  (Random House, 1998)

- ◎ **Day of the Dragon King**
  (Random House, 1998)

- ◎ **Viking Ships at Sunrise**
  (Random House, 1998)

- ◎ **Hour of the Olympics**
  (Random House, 1998)

Students might be interested to know that the author says this cluster is her favorite. Jack and Annie explore ancient times in this cluster, traveling from Pompeii to China, Ireland, and Greece. As they visit ancient civilizations, they save certain books from being destroyed. They are subsequently rescued by mythological characters from those saved books. After they learn that each character is an actual constellation in the night sky, Morgan reassures them that the "old stories are always with us—we are never alone."

Catching the Clues

For their first mission as master librarians, Jack and Annie must go back in time and save books from libraries that were lost in history. In *Vacation Under the Volcano*, they escape Mount Vesuvius in Pompeii with a scroll called The Strongest Man on Earth. They save an ancient Chinese bamboo book in *Day of the Dragon King*, and a manuscript made by ancient Irish monks in *Viking Ships at Sunrise*. Finally, they're given an ancient Greek scroll in *Hour of the Olympics*.

Fact Finders Scavenger Hunt

The books in this cluster take children back to ancient times. This scavenger hunt lets children take a closer look at life long ago. To set up the scavenger hunt, copy the questions below on the chalkboard or make photocopies for children. Use the answers as a springboard for further investigation. If a research guide is available, have students use the index to look up additional information on each answer.

1. If you lived during the Roman Empire and wanted to know the future, who would you ask? (*a soothsayer*)

2. If you lived in the time of the Dragon King, would you have been encouraged to read and write? Why? (*no; the emperor thought reading and writing gave people too much power*)

3. If you lived in the time of the Vikings, what would you use instead of paper and pencil? (*sheepskin, goose quills, paints made of earth and plants*)

4. What Olympic event from ancient Greece is not part of the modern day games? (*chariot races*)

5. What mythological creatures from each of the four books in Cluster 4 do Jack and Annie see in the constellations? (*Hercules, the silk weaver, the serpent monster, and Pegasus*)

Vacation Under the Volcano

Before You Read

Show students a map of the world and locate Italy. Can students find the city of Pompeii? (The map will not show Pompeii.) Inform students that there once was a city in Italy called Pompeii. Point out its former location southeast of Naples. Ask students to make predictions about why this city no longer exists. Explain that this ancient city was buried by a volcanic eruption.

After You Read

Erupting Volcanoes
(Science and Language Arts)

Jack and Annie observe Mount Vesuvius erupt. Let students build their own volcanoes to explore the science behind volcanoes. Here's a twist on the familiar setup:

- Divide the class into groups. Give each group a tray, vinegar, baking soda, water, a small plastic bottle, a funnel, red food coloring, and sand. Have each group devise a demonstration of an erupting volcano. When students are satisfied with their plans, have them write a step-by-step how-to plan.

- Let groups trade plans, and follow the directions to make a volcano. Which plans were successful? Discuss any problems in the steps. Then challenge children to create an experiment that would result in a more/less quiet eruption. Test their ideas!

- In discussing results, guide students to understand that the baking soda's gas rose and pushed the liquid out with it. Likewise, in a real volcano, the gases in the chamber build up. When they are released through the chamber and out of the volcano, they push the melted rock out, too.

Race of the Roman Numerals (Math)

The setting of *Vacation Under the Volcano* is ancient Rome. Learn about the Roman numeration system with this game. As a warm-up, brainstorm places students have seen Roman numerals—for example, on clocks and in books. Review what each symbol stands for. (*I-1; V-5; X-10; L-50; C-100; D-500; M-1000*)

- Give each pair of children a copy of the game board (page 41), a game chip, and paper and pencil.

- Have players take turns flicking the chip from *Start* to any spot on the board and recording the sum of all the spaces the chip touches. If the chip goes off the board, players may agree to a second try. The goal is to flick the chip on the combination of Roman numerals that will yield the highest sum.

Shopping in Pompeii
(Math and Social Studies)

While Jack and Annie explore the ancient town of Pompeii, they come across many types of shops, including clothing stores, fish shops, barbershops, and bakeries. Jack notices that it's not very different from the way some people today shop. Do students agree? Ask students if they know the name for a book that helps people find businesses (or services). Share the yellow pages of a directory. To review this reference book, let children take turns naming items to buy (or services they need) and locating the listings. For additional practice, publish a directory for the city of Pompeii, using shops from the story and others students think would fit. Review the concept of alphabetical order before having students complete their final drafts and put their directory pages together.

Race of the Roman Numerals

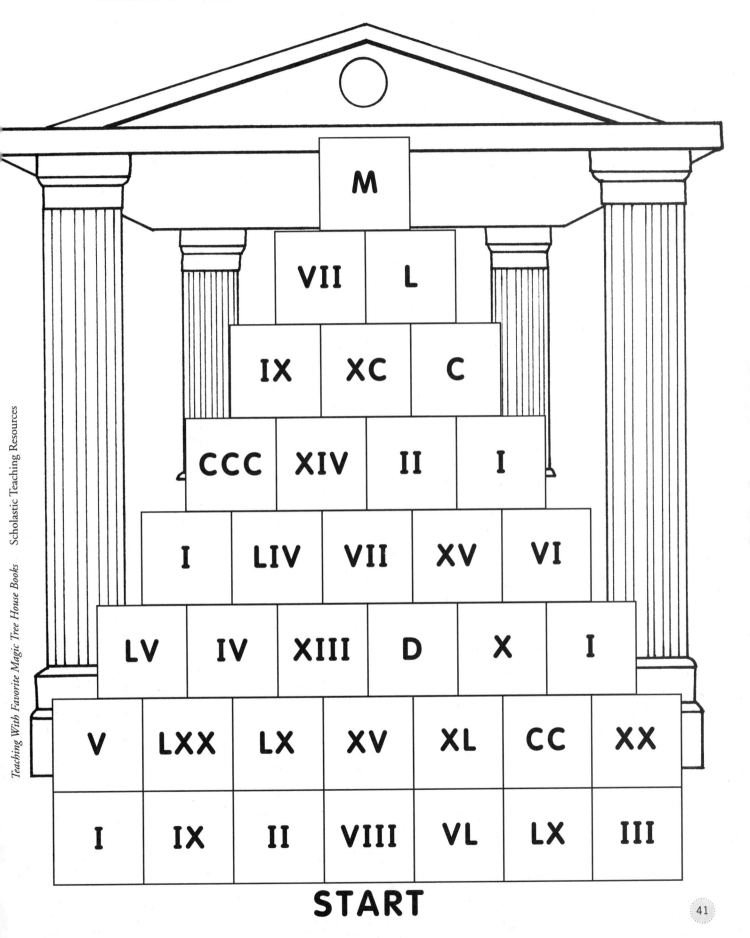

M

VII L

IX XC C

CCC XIV II I

I LIV VII XV VI

LV IV XIII D X I

V LXX LX XV XL CC XX

I IX II VIII VL LX III

START

Day of the Dragon King

Jack and Annie visit ancient China, where the emperor has ordered the burning of all books because he does not want his subjects learning about things unless he wants them to. Discuss with students the power of words and what a book can teach you. Ask students to share books they feel are important to them and why.

After You Read

Great Wall of China Challenge (Math)

Jack and Annie traveled on part of the Great Wall of China. The wall was built more than 2,000 years ago, took more than 200 years to complete, and is 3,700 miles long. Help students comprehend the wall's enormous length with this activity:

- Take students outside to a large playground area or field. Have students lie down head to toe. When everyone is lying down, mark the beginning and ending point. Have students get up and measure the distance in feet.

- Ask students to predict how many of their combined lengths it would take to equal the wall's length. Record estimates.

- Guide students in calculating the answer by multiplying the number of miles (3,700) by the number of feet in a mile (5,280). Divide the answer (19,536,000 feet) by the combined length of students.

Bamboo Strip Book (Language Arts)

Jack and Annie save a bamboo book from the fire. Bamboo is a tropical woody grass with hard stems. Long ago, books were written on bamboo strips. Writers used a brush and ink, and started at the top of the strip and worked their way to the bottom. When there were enough strips to make a book, the strips were put in order horizontally and tied together. The book could be rolled up for easy carrying. Students can make a simple bamboo book with craft sticks, glue, and yarn. Have them write on the sticks from top to bottom. When they are finished writing, have them turn over the sticks and place them side by side in order. Have students glue three pieces of yarn across the back: one across the top of the sticks, one across the bottom, and one in the middle. When the glue dries, students can roll up the book and carry it home.

Chinese Counting (Math)

Morgan gives Jack and Annie a bamboo stick with the title of the story they must find. The title is written vertically and is made up of characters that represent different things or ideas. Students can practice Chinese writing with page 43. Have children look at and trace each Chinese number from one to ten. Have children copy the Chinese numbers in the space provided. For more practice, students can complete the information on the side of the page, filling in their age, grade, and so on.

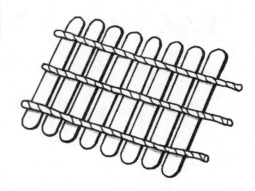

Number	Chinese Number	Your Turn!
1	一	
2	二	
3	三	
4	四	
5	五	
6	六	
7	七	
8	八	
9	九	
10	十	

Name _____

Date _____

Chinese Counting

Your age: _____

Your grade: _____

How many feet tall you are
(to the nearest foot):

_____

How many days in one week:

_____

Another number you know
(like your favorite number):

_____

Teaching With Favorite Magic Tree House Books   Scholastic Teaching Resources

Viking Ships at Sunrise

Before You Read

Jack and Annie are off to save another book for Morgan's library. This time they have to face Vikings in ancient Ireland. At this time in history every book that was written was done by hand. This was a painstaking and time-consuming task that was mostly performed by monks. Invite students to time how long it takes to copy a page from a favorite chapter book. Now multiply that number by the number of pages. What a long process!

After You Read

A Shipshape Classroom
(Social Studies and Language Arts)

Vikings were master shipbuilders. Annie and Jack accidentally go for a sail in one of the Viking ships. Turn the classroom into a Viking ship to learn about basic boat anatomy and vocabulary.

- Using the book as a resource, have students name parts of a ship (such as bow, stern, port, starboard, and helm).

- Use colorful electrical tape to mark off a "ship" in the classroom (incorporating as much of the classroom as possible). Have students use sentence strips or large index cards to label the different parts of the ship, such as the bow (the front of the classroom), the stern (the back of the classroom), port (left side), starboard (right side), and helm (the teacher's desk).

- Play a game to reinforce vocabulary. Have children gather together in one part of the ship. Call out another part of the ship. Have students quickly gather there. Continue, calling students to different parts of the ship. As

a challenge, remove the labels and repeat the game. Can students remember where each part is in relation to other parts?

Viking Vocabulary
(Social Studies and Language Arts)

Can students name at least ten parts of a Viking warrior? Let them try, with an activity that reinforces content-area vocabulary and teaches how to use diagrams as a nonfiction tool. Divide the class into small groups. Give each group a Magic Tree House research guide. Ask students to locate a diagram in the guide. Have them share with the class the purpose for the diagram (for example, to show the parts of a knight's armor). Ask them to make one inference based on the information in the diagram (for example, there were so many pieces to a suit of armor, a knight would have to plan ahead to get dressed). Let children create their own diagram to learn more. Give each child a copy of page 45. Have students use what they learned in the book and other Viking resources to label each part of the diagram. Have children give the diagram a title and write

a caption that includes an inference they can make from the information in the diagram.

Vikings Internet Scavenger Hunt
(Language Arts and Art)

Jack and Annie learn a lot about the Vikings, including the fact that they were scavengers who raided and stole. Invite students to go on their own scavenger hunt—on the Internet! Give each child a copy of the following scavenger hunt items:

- Write your name in runes (the Viking language).

- Design your own Viking ship's prow (the fore part of a vessel).

- Find the most impressive Viking fact you can.

Bookmark Web site addresses to guide the search. (See Resources, pages 15–16.) Before proceeding with the scavenger hunt, review guidelines for Internet safety. To go further, combine students' most impressive facts into a question and answer guide to Vikings, a great activity for reinforcing nonfiction writing skills.

Name _____   Date _____

Viking
Vocabulary

Teaching With Favorite Magic Tree House Books   Scholastic Teaching Resources

Hour of the Olympics

Before You Read

Jack and Annie go back to ancient Greece, where they both intend to see the Olympics, but Annie is in for a surprise when she finds out that girls are not allowed! Ask students if they know about any other cases in history where girls and women may not have been allowed to participate in something, such as voting. Discuss how women's rights have changed over time (and who has helped lead the movement, including Susan B. Anthony).

After You Read

Olympic Word Problems (Math)

Invite students to take Jack and Annie's Olympic adventure further with an activity that uses numbers as a springboard.

● Have students research ancient and modern Olympics, focusing on facts that involve numbers—for example, "Women were first allowed to participate in the Olympics in 1912." (They were allowed to compete in swimming.)

● Display the facts. Then let students create word problems with them—for example, "Women were first allowed to participate in the Olympics in 1912. How many years have women been in the Olympics?"

● Have students write and illustrate their problems on one side of a large index card and the answer on the other. Students can take turns solving one another's problems and checking their answers on the back.

Gods and Goddesses Peek-Through Posters

(Language Arts and Social Studies)

Jack and Annie learn about mythological characters as they explore ancient Greece. Encourage students to discover for themselves the attributes and powers of the ancient Greek gods and goddesses. First, compile a list of the most widely known of the gods and goddesses. Then have students choose one to research. For a fun display, follow these steps:

● Give each child a sheet of posterboard. Have children draw a picture of their god or goddess, including appropriate details and clothing, but leaving the face blank.

● Help students cut a hole in the poster where the face appears. This will serve as a peek-through spot for the student's head. One at a time, have students give speeches as the character they have researched, revealing important details except the name. Students can

try to guess who the god or goddess is, using the clues provided in the speech and on the peek-through poster.

Olympic Day (Math, Movement, and Dramatic Play)

Host your own Olympics by simulating some of the ancient Olympic events and tying them in with math. You'll need a large, safe area, and materials for the following four stations: long jump (colorful electrical tape to make the starting line), discus (a plastic or foam flying disc to throw), 20-yard dash (something to mark the start and finish line), and the javelin (a foam football with a "tail"). Divide the class into four groups and have students rotate through each station to try their hand at these Olympic events. Use various measuring tools to keep track of students' distances and times. It's handy to tape a record sheet to the back of students' shirts to record the personal records they set!

- ◎ **Tonight on the Titanic**
  (Random House, 1999)

- ◎ **Buffalo Before Breakfast**
  (Random House, 1999)

- ◎ **Tigers at Twilight**
  (Random House, 1999)

- ◎ **Dingoes at Dinnertime**
  (Random House, 1999)

Jack and Annie call on their bravery and courage as they encounter some dangerous situations: They are aboard the sinking *Titanic*, are stalked by a wild tiger, must escape a wildfire in an Australian forest, and get in the middle of a buffalo stampede. Somehow the adventurous brother and sister escape disaster and break the magic spell.

Catching the Clues

When Jack and Annie go up into the tree house one stormy night, they have a surprise visitor. It's a dog with a note. The note explains that he is under a spell and to free him the kids must get four special things: a gift from a ship lost at sea, a gift from a prairie blue, a gift from a forest far away, and a gift from a kangaroo. In *Tonight on the Titanic*, Jack and Annie are given a pocket watch from Lucy and William, two children getting on a lifeboat. Grandmother from the Lakota tribe gives the kids a brown-and-white feather for their courage in *Buffalo Before Breakfast*. A lotus flower is a gift from a blind hermit in the jungle for helping to save a tiger in *Tigers at Twilight*. The last gift comes from a mother kangaroo—a piece of bark with a rainbow serpent painted on it. The four gifts release the dog from the spell, and the dog turns out to be a boy who works in Morgan's library!

Fact Finders Scavenger Hunt

This scavenger hunt sharpens students' understanding of some of the amazing things Jack and Annie discover in this cluster. To set up the scavenger hunt, copy the questions below on the chalkboard or make photocopies for children. Use the answers as a springboard for further investigation. If a research guide is available, have students use the index to look up additional information on each answer.

1. How long did it take the huge *Titanic* to sink? (*It hit the iceberg at 11:40 P.M. and sank about 2:20 A.M.—2 hours and 40 minutes later.*)

2. After the *Titanic* sank, what law was changed to protect passengers on ships? (*Ships had to have enough lifeboats to carry all passengers.*)

3. In the early 1800s there were 40 million bison on the Great Plains. How many were left 100 years later? (*less than 300*)

4. A python is not poisonous. Does that mean it's safe? Why? (*No. It squeezes its prey to death and swallows it whole.*)

5. Why are wildfires especially dangerous to koalas? (*They are slow-moving animals and can't escape.*)

Tonight on the Titanic

Before You Read

Brainstorm modes of transportation, such as on foot, bicycle, automobile, airplane, boat, horse, wagon, truck, and skateboard. Sort the items into two groups: Transportation Today and Transportation 100 Years Ago. Do some belong on both lists? Explain that, during the time of the *Titanic*, automobiles and planes were relatively new and many people traveled by ship to reach faraway destinations.

After You Read

Send a Telegraph
(Social Studies and Language Arts)

Jack and Annie anxiously watch the ship's wireless operator sending emergency telegraphs after it hit the iceberg. Have students use the dictionary and other reference materials to learn about telegraphs. (Using Morse code, letters—represented by a combination of dots and dashes—were transmitted as short or long electrical connections to compose a message.) Give each child a copy of page 49. Let students use Morse code to compose and tap out messages to one another.

A *Titanic* Quiz
(Social Studies)

The *Titanic* was the biggest ship in the world. The book includes some facts about this palatial ship, the research guide more. Instead of giving students a quiz on what they learn, let them help write one! Model the activity by writing a sample multiple choice question on the chalkboard. Include a distracter

as a possible answer. Discuss each answer, reviewing distracters in particular. For example, if a question requires students to subtract and they add instead, they might find their answer, though incorrect, among the choices. Give each student a copy of page 50. Have students provide three choices for each question, including the correct answer and one distracter. Display quizzes with answer keys tucked underneath for self-checking.

The Tip of the Iceberg
(Science)

If the word *berg* means "mountain" in German, what does the word *iceberg* mean? (*mountain of ice*) Let students learn more about icebergs with a simple experiment.

- Place one ice cube in a clear glass of water and another in a clear glass of purple grape juice. What do students observe? (*Most of the ice in the water is visible, even under the water. Only the tip of the ice is visible in the grape juice.*)

- Ask: "Which glass is like the dark waters of the sea?" Explain that, like the ice in the dark liquid, only a small part of an iceberg can be seen above water. There is a mountain of ice underwater—eight times as much! That's what makes icebergs dangerous to ships. Now, what do students think the expression "the tip of the iceberg" means?

Titanic
by Will Osborne and Mary Pope Osborne
(Random House, 2002)

This reference includes diagrams and drawings of the *Titanic*. It also features photographs—a primary source that can provide students with additional information. Compare these features of nonfiction books. For example, have students compare the photo of the *Titanic* on page 42 with the diagrams on pages 22-25. Can they locate in the photo the places labeled in the diagrams? Can students use the diagrams to identify the location of the drawing on pages 46-47?

Name _____ Date _____

Morse Code

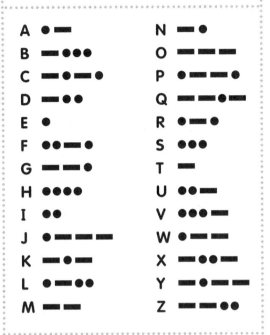

A	●▬	N	▬●
B	▬●●●	O	▬▬▬
C	▬●▬●	P	●▬▬●
D	▬●●	Q	▬▬●▬
E	●	R	●▬●
F	●●▬●	S	●●●
G	▬▬●	T	▬
H	●●●●	U	●●▬
I	●●	V	●●●▬
J	●▬▬▬	W	●▬▬
K	▬●▬	X	▬●●▬
L	●▬●●	Y	▬●▬▬
M	▬▬	Z	▬▬●●

Send a Telegraph

Compose a message here. Then tap it out for a partner to decode. Pause between each letter and word to help your listener decode your message.

_____

_____

_____

_____

_____

_____

_____

Name _____ Date _____

A Titanic Quiz

1. A football field is 300 feet long. The *Titanic* was as long as three football fields! That's about as long as:

   A. _____

   B. _____

   C. _____

2. The *Titanic* was as tall as an 11-story building. If one story is 10 feet, how tall was the *Titanic*?

   A. _____

   B. _____

   C. _____

3. The *Titanic* could hold 2,500 people. That's about as many people as:

   A. _____

   B. _____

   C. _____

4. A first-class room on the *Titanic* was 50 feet long. How does this compare with how long the classroom is?

   A. _____

   B. _____

   C. _____

5. The *Titanic* had the largest room of any ship—the dining room. It could seat 550 people! To seat them all, it would take:

   A. _____ four-person tables.

   B. _____ four-person tables.

   C. _____ four-person tables.

Teaching With Favorite Magic Tree House Books Scholastic Teaching Resources

Buffalo Before Breakfast

Before You Read

In the foreword to this book, Mary Pope Osborne shares that it was difficult writing about the Lakota Indians because there were several groups of this tribe. To help students get a feel for the research that often goes into writing fiction, have students research information about various Lakota groups. Compile information on chart paper for easy reference. As students read the book, have them notice which facts the author used.

After You Read

Strong Like a Bear
(Language Arts and Art)

Jack and Annie see a Lakota woman sewing bear claws, hawk feathers, and porcupine quills onto a shirt. Grandmother explains that this will give her the strength of the animals. Brainstorm a list of animals and their traits—for example, fox-cunning; bear-strong; and deer-fast. Let children make a vest that will give them the "strength" of these animals.

- Give each child a brown paper grocery bag. Have children turn the opened bag upside down and cut up the center of the front of the bag, continuing halfway through the bottom of the bag (to create the front opening of the vest).

- Help students cut an opening

on the bottom to fit their head and armholes on the sides.

- Let students decorate their vests by drawing features of the animals that will give them strength.

Then and Now (Social Studies and Language Arts)

Jack and Annie discover many differences between the Lakota world and their own. Have students follow these directions to make accordion-fold books for comparing and contrasting Lakota life to their own:

- Cut a sheet of 12- by-18-inch paper in half lengthwise and tape the two pieces end to end. Fold the strip in half end-to-end, and fold it in half two more times to make eight panels. Draw lines along each crease.

- Write "Lakota Life" on the first section of one side and use the remaining sections to record facts about school, homes, animals, and so on. Turn the paper over and repeat for "My Life." Fold back and forth on the creases to create an accordion fold book that tells two stories.

The Buffalo's Gifts
(Science and Language Arts)

When Jack and Annie ask Black Hawk's grandmother why he hunts buffaloes, she tells them that the buffalo

Buffalo
skin- teepee
bones- tools
horns- cups
hair- ropes
ribs- sleds

gives the Lakota people many gifts. Jack makes a list of them (see above). Ask students why they think Jack included the information on a list instead of a paragraph. Explain that a list is a quick way to record information. Brainstorm lists that people write, such as grocery lists, and "to do" lists. Write some fun list topics on slips of paper, such as "things that start with the same first letter as your name," "things in the classroom that are red," "things that are round," and "words that begin with the letters *sw-.*" Set a timer for one minute, select a topic randomly, and let children make a list! Compare lists and discuss how list-writing can help children be more efficient with some class assignments, such as research projects.

Tigers at Twilight

Before You Read

Introduce students to new vocabulary such as *extinct, endangered, poachers,* and *wildlife protection.* Discuss the definition of each. As students read the book, ask them if they have anything to add to their definitions, based on what they've learned.

After You Read

Sound Safari

(Language Arts and Science)

The hermit Jack and Annie meet is blind, but he learns about the world around him by listening. Have students practice listening skills by going on a sound safari around school.

- Before setting out on the sound safari, agree on places to stop and listen—for example, the cafeteria, the gymnasium, the main office, the nurse's office, the playground, the classroom, the library, and the music room.

- Gather students and provide them with clipboards, paper, and pencils. Set off for each designated spot, and let children listen and record sounds they hear.

- Back in the classroom, compile results. Which place was noisiest? Quietest?

Save the Animals

(Science and Art)

Jack and Annie meet two animals that are in danger of becoming extinct: the tiger and rhinoceros. Explore the concept of extinction by having students create posters designed to increase awareness of animals that are endangered. Have students use reference materials to gather facts and pictures to use on their posters—for example, "There were 40,000 tigers in India in the 1800s. Today there are only about 4,000!" Encourage students to recognize that although they can't stop, say, the poaching of tigers themselves, increasing awareness of a problem—for example, through displaying informative posters—is one way to help.

The Best Beginnings

(Language Arts)

Ask students how the story begins. (*with Jack and Annie talking*) Dialogue is an attention-getting way to begin a story. In the case of *Tigers at Twilight,* the use of dialogue lets readers imagine right from the start that they're walking and talking with Jack and Annie as they get ready for a new adventure. Explore other techniques Mary Pope Osborne uses to begin Magic Tree House books. For example, the following books use sound effects:

Buffalo Before Breakfast:
"Arf! Arf! Arf!"

Good Morning, Gorillas:
"Tap-tap-tap."

Polar Bears Past Bedtime:
"Whoo."

Let students experiment with these techniques by rewriting the beginning of a Magic Tree House book that does not use dialogue or sound effects. Have students first decide which technique would be most effective. Then have them rewrite the first page or two to try it out. Encourage children to notice what they like about other beginnings and to try out some of those techniques in their own writing.

Dingoes at Dinnertime

Before You Read

In this adventure, Jack and Annie are whisked away to Australia to retrieve the final gift that will break the spell of an enchanted dog. There they learn about Australian wildlife and help save a koala and baby joey from a wildfire. Have students locate Australia on a globe. Discuss why it is sometimes referred to as "down under."

After You Read

Kangaroo Count (Math)

Kangaroos are so numerous in Australia that for every person there are ten kangaroos. (There are about 19 million people living in Australia.) Have students devise simple math problems to figure out how many kangaroos there are for a given number of people.

Example: "If there are 17 people, how many kangaroos would there be?" Provide students with manipulatives to help illustrate the problems.

Compass Points

(Social Studies)

Annie and Jack could have used a compass to locate the spot where they first found the joey. Divide the class into three or four groups. Provide each group with a clear glass filled with water, a quarter-inch slice from the end of a cork, a magnet, and a sewing needle. Guide children in following these steps:

- Float the cork in the glass of water.

- Rub the needle over the magnet in the same direction about 50 times, and then lay the needle on the cork.

Have students walk around the room to observe the direction each needle is facing. (*They'll all be facing the same way.*) Ask students to try to point the cork in another direction. (*It will always point in the same direction. This happens because once the needle is magnetized, it lines up with Earth's north and south magnetic poles, working just like a compass.*)

Publish a Nonfiction Companion

(Language Arts and Social Studies)

From being the only country that occupies a whole continent to being home to 170 different marsupials, Australia is an interesting place to investigate. Let children learn more by making a mini-research guide, modeled after the Magic Tree House nonfiction companions that Mary Pope Osborne and Will Osborne write. Together, look through a couple of Magic Tree House research guides and list special features, such as diagrams, charts, pictures, definitions, pronunciation keys, and indexes. Let each child choose a research topic—for example, any of the marsupials, the country's size, Aborigine myths, and the dingo. Have children use the research books as inspiration to decide how to present their information. Encourage them to use a combination of features to make the information clear. Put the pages together with a table of contents and index to make a Magic Tree House research guide.

- ◎ **Civil War on Sunday**
  (Random House, 2000)

- ◎ **Revolutionary War on Wednesday**
  (Random House, 2000)

- ◎ **Twister on Tuesday**
  (Random House, 2001)

- ◎ **Earthquake in the Early Morning**
  (Random House, 2001)

Mary Pope Osborne got the idea for the first book in this cluster from a fan who won a Magic Tree House writing contest. This cluster starts with two journeys back in American history and ends up with two dangerous forces of nature. In *Civil War on Sunday*, Jack and Annie meet up with Clara Barton on the front lines of the U.S. Civil War. In *Revolutionary War on Wednesday*, they meet up with George Washington. In *Twister on Tuesday*, they have to survive a twister that rampages through the U.S. prairies of the 1870s. In *Earthquake in the Early Morning*, they have to battle the 1906 San Francisco earthquake.

Catching the Clues

In this cluster, Jack and Annie must help save Camelot by finding four special types of writing: "Something to follow, Something to send, Something to learn, Something to lend." In *Civil War on Sunday*, the kids meet famous nurse Clara Barton, who gives them a list of rules to follow. A captain in the Continental Army gives them a letter to send to his family in *Revolutionary War on Wednesday*. A poem written on a slate from a pioneer schoolhouse proves to be the "something to learn" in *Twister on Tuesday*. Finally, the two lend hope with a sign during the San Francisco earthquake.

Fact Finders Scavenger Hunt

Guide children to recognize how history shapes the world today with this scavenger hunt. To set up the scavenger hunt, copy the questions below on the chalkboard or make photocopies for children. Use the answers as a springboard for further investigation. If a research guide is available, have students use the index to look up additional information on each answer.

1. What disagreement led the North and South into war? (*the issue of ending slavery*)

2. What does the Civil War teach Jack about helping people? (*for example, when someone is hurt, you help, no matter who the person is*)

3. In his speech to the troops, General Washington read the words of what other famous patriot? (*Thomas Paine*)

4. What are three hardships pioneers faced on the prairie? (*storms, grasshopper plagues, and lost crops*)

5. What disaster happened as a result of the 1906 San Francisco earthquake? (*a fire that lasted for three days*)

Civil War on Sunday

Before You Read

Jack and Annie meet up with Clara Barton on the front lines of the U.S. Civil War. Ask students what they know about the Civil War. List their ideas on a KWL chart. After students create the "Know" part of the chart, share background information about the Civil War. Circle or cross out ideas. Follow up by letting students share what they would like to know. Encourage them to look for that information as they read.

After You Read

Clara's Comfort
(Language Arts)

Clara Barton gives Jack and Annie a list of things they can do to help the Civil War soldiers:

"Be cheerful.

Lessen sorrow and give hope.

Be brave.

Put aside your own feelings.

Don't give up."

To deepen students' understanding of what they read, and give them an opportunity to respond, let them act out ways in which Jack and Annie did what Clara asked. Divide the class into five groups. Assign each group one of the items on the list. Have students reread passages from the book to find ways Jack and Annie helped the soldiers. To do this, they will need to use what Jack and Annie say and do, as well as make inferences based on both. For example, Jack groans when Annie tells him to get the water bucket. Then he reads the first line of the list ("Be cheerful."), picks up the bucket, and tries to smile. Students will need to decide how his posture and expression might have changed as they act out this moment.

Letters From the Past
(Language Arts)

Encourage children to relate to what they read, explore point of view, and make inferences with an activity that reinforces letter-writing skills. Ask children to name people involved with the Civil War—for example, Clara Barton, Abe Lincoln, characters from the book, young soldiers, worried family members of soldiers, and slaves. Invite children to imagine the thoughts and feelings these people had about the war. Pair up children for a letter-writing exchange. Have children write letters to each other from the point of view of a person on the list. Have partners "send" their letters to each other and write responses. For example, Clara Barton might exchange letters with a soldier's worried family. Children can age the paper they write on by staining it lightly with tea (letting it dry before they write on it) and crumpling the edges.

Beat of the Drum
(Music and Movement)

The author's note mentions that nearly 60,000 boys served as drummer boys or buglers in the Civil War. Drummers used different drumbeats as signals to give soldiers their orders. Have children make their own Civil War drums by covering coffee cans or oatmeal canisters (lids on) with construction paper. Brainstorm classroom transitions, such as meeting, cleanup, and lunch. Come up with different drumbeats to signal each time. Students can return the beat to signal that they heard.

Revolutionary War on Wednesday

Jack and Annie meet up with George Washington during the American Revolution. Show students Emanuel Leutze's famous painting *Washington Crossing the Delaware* (1851). Ask students to describe what is happening in it. Compare the painting with the book cover. Share the author's note, which discusses historical inaccuracies in the painting.

George Washington and Me (Language Arts)

Jack and Annie are in awe when they look up and realize they are seeing the great George Washington. Today we still look up to him as one of our greatest American heroes.

Invite students to compare themselves with George Washington. Give each child a copy of page 57. Have children complete the information for items 1–5. Then have them add a new comparison, based on something else they know about George Washington.

Powerful Words

(Language Arts)

"The harder the conflict, the more glorious the triumph...." Jack and Annie get to hear George Washington deliver a passionate speech to a crowd of soldiers. Bring this speech to life in the classroom by letting children take turns reading it aloud. (Copy it on parchment-like paper for added effect.) To reinforce speaking skills, encourage children to think about George Washington's audience and the reason for his speech. What kind of voice do they think George Washington used when he delivered this speech? Encourage reading fluency by providing time to practice the speech before delivering it. Follow up by inviting students to deliver an original speech about something they feel strongly about, such as protecting the environment or putting an end to bullying. Discuss what makes a speech effective—for example, a beginning that makes listeners want to keep listening, and an ending that sticks with listeners long after the speech is finished.

Time Marches On (Math)

Jack finds several important dates corresponding to the Revolutionary War. Students can find more important dates in the author's notes in the back of the book. Using this information as well as other research material, create a class time line of events that occurred leading up to, and including, the Revolutionary War. To add a twist to this activity, provide students with the facts (but not the dates) in the morning message. Challenge children to research where that fact belongs on the time line and write their answers below the message under sticky notes. Encourage them to note their sources, as well. (They'll get good practice using the index of a reference book and crediting sources.)

Name _____ Date _____

George Washington and Me

Paste your picture here.

All About George Washington

All About Me

① George was born on a farm in Virginia.

① I was born _____ .

② George always showed good manners.

② I show good manners by _____ .

③ One of George's best traits was that he was an honest man.

③ One of the best things about me is _____ .

④ George loved to ride his horses.

④ I love to _____ .

⑤ George Washington believed that hard work paid off.

⑤ I believe _____ .

⑥ A new fact about George Washington is:

_____ .

⑥ A new fact about me is:

_____ .

Twister on Tuesday

Before You Read

Jack and Annie are whisked back to a prairie in the 1870s, where they survive a twister! Explain that part of the setting is a one-room schoolhouse, which children of all ages attended together. Ask students to think about differences between a one-room schoolhouse and their school. Discuss possible difficulties of having one teacher in one room for students of all ages.

After You Read

My McGuffey Reader
(Language Arts)

Jack and Annie read poems from a McGuffey Reader, the most popular school book in the 1880s. Created by a teacher named McGuffey, it consisted of poems, stories, and famous sayings and was used to teach children how to read. Create a class version of the McGuffey Reader. Have each student select a favorite poem, short story, or famous saying and write it on a sheet of paper. Compile students' selections, add a cover, and bind to make an addition to the class library that showcases each child's contributions.

Create a Slate (Social Studies, Language Arts, and Art)

When Jack and Annie visit the one-room schoolhouse, they are given a slate for writing instead of paper. Let children share this experience by creating a "slate" writing board. Give each student a sheet of construction paper and some craft sticks. Have children glue the craft sticks around the edge of the paper to create a frame. When dry, students can use chalk to copy a favorite poem, perform a math problem, or write a fact about pioneer life.

Make a Twister (Science)

Guide children to notice the shape of the twister on the cover of the book. (*funnel*) Let students make a "twister" to see this spinning action. Fill a clear jar almost to the top with water. Add a teaspoon of liquid dish detergent, three drops of red food coloring, and a marble. Secure the lid. Let students take turns moving the jar in a quick, circular motion. Place the jar on a flat surface and observe the "twister." Compare what is happening in the jar to the twister on the book cover. (*They each have a swirling funnel shape.*) Discuss what causes wind to swirl in this way. (*Tornadoes develop when a strong wind from one direction blows over wind from another direction. The winds roll over each other and make the air spin like a top.*)

Twisters and Other Terrible Storms
by Will Osborne and Mary Pope Osborne
(Random House, 2003)

This guide covers wind, clouds, lightning, hurricanes, blizzards, twisters, and other stormy weather conditions. Within those topics are dozens of content-area vocabulary words. Strengthen vocabulary and enhance understanding of the subject matter with a Stormy Weather Word Wall. List weather words, such as *cumulonimbus clouds, lightning, tornado,* and *blizzard*. Have each child choose a word, cut out tagboard in a shape that helps illustrate the meaning, and write a definition. Hang from the ceiling to create a stormy weather word display.

Earthquake in the Early Morning

The earth beneath Jack and Annie's feet rumbles and shakes as they end up in San Francisco in 1906. The most famous earthquake ever is beginning, and Jack and Annie have to find the final writing needed to help Morgan le Fay save Camelot. Ask students if they have ever seen movies or photos of what an earthquake looks like and the damage one can do.

Testing the Richter Scale (Science)

Jack and Annie feel the impact of an earthquake—the ground shakes and moves. Scientists measure how much the ground shakes during an earthquake with an instrument called a Richter scale. To demonstrate how the Richter scale works, try this hands-on activity.

- Assign each student a partner. Have each pair of children tape a long strip of paper to the surface of a desk. Have one partner stand next to the desk, while the other sits at the desk.

- Explain to students that you will call out numbers from one to ten. As each number is called, the partner who is standing will hit the desk with a fist. One will be the lightest bang while ten will be the hardest. Demonstrate these levels so that children stay within reasonable limits.

- While their partners are hitting the desk, seated students try to draw a straight line on the strip of paper.

- Guide students to observe that as the number on the scale goes up, the lines on the paper become more squiggly. Explain that, like the lines on the paper, the movement of the lines on the Richter scale measures how intense an earthquake is. The more drastic the jumps, the bigger the earthquake.

Earthquake Safety
(Social Studies and Movement)

As Jack and Annie walk around San Francisco after the earthquake, they see destruction and danger. Today people in earthquake-prone areas are more prepared. One of the rules for those inside a building is called Duck, Cover, and Hold. Practice this safety tip with a mock earthquake drill. Play music to signal the start of the earthquake. When students hear it, they drop to the floor wherever they are, find a desk or other piece of furniture that they can safely crawl under, and hold onto that piece of furniture until the earthquake (the music) stops. Repeat this procedure for different lengths of time.

Read All About It
(Language Arts)

While walking through the rubble left behind after the San Francisco earthquake, Jack and Annie meet a newspaper reporter and a photographer whose stories and pictures helped tell the story of the earthquake. Discuss how newspapers help people get information. Invite students to learn more about newspapers with a scavenger hunt. For example, challenge children to:

- Find a headline.
- Find the publishing date.
- Find tomorrow's weather.
- Find a reporter's byline.
- Find a local story.
- Find a news story about another country.
- Find the score of a sports game.
- Find a caption.

◎ **Stage Fright on a Summer Night**
(Random House, 2002)

◎ **Good Morning, Gorillas**
(Random House, 2002)

◎ **Thanksgiving on Thursday**
(Random House, 2002)

◎ **High Tide in Hawaii**
(Random House, 2003)

In this cluster, the brother and sister team travel back in time and around the world to find special magic. They learn the magic of words from William Shakespeare and the magic of communication without words from a gorilla using sign language. They learn life lessons about caring for others from Squanto and from Boka and Kama, two Hawaiian children.

Catching the Clues

On their latest adventure, Jack and Annie must find four special kinds of magic. At the beginning of each adventure, they are given a rhyme that will help them find the special magic. They discover the magic of theater as they act in the Globe Theatre with William Shakespeare in *Stage Fright on a Summer Night*. They discover the magic of animals when they communicate in sign language with a gorilla in *Good Morning, Gorillas*. They discover the magic of community when they travel back in time to the first Thanksgiving in *Thanksgiving on Thursday*. Last, Jack and Annie discover the magic of friendship in *High Tide in Hawaii*.

Fact Finders Scavenger Hunt

The answers to these scavenger hunt questions have something in common: they're all about communication. To set up the scavenger hunt, copy the questions below on the chalkboard or make photocopies for children. Use the answers as a springboard for further investigation. If a research guide is available, have students use the index to look up additional information on each answer.

(1) What three words did William Shakespeare invent that we use today to tell direction or position? (*forward, downstairs, upstairs*)

(2) How did a gorilla learn to communicate with humans? (*with sign language*)

(3) What sound did Jack borrow from the gorillas to scare off a leopard? (*a loud hooting sound*)

(4) What word did pilgrims use for *you*? (*thou*)

(5) How did the early Hawaiians communicate? (*with hula dancing*)

Stage Fright on a Summer Night

Before You Read

Jack and Annie travel back in time to Elizabethan England where they see the London Bridge and the famous Globe Theatre—along with the man who built it, William Shakespeare! Ask students about their experiences with performances like plays. Have they been in a play? Been to see one? Brainstorm words that correspond to plays or other productions, such as *actors, scenery, scripts, roles, audience,* and *theater.* Students can look for other words as they read the story.

After You Read

Diagramming the Globe (Math)

Jack and Annie perform at the Globe Theatre, Shakespeare's famous theater. Although this famous theater no longer exists, a replica was recently built. The theater was built in the shape of a circle—almost! It was actually built in the shape of 20 straight lines connected to form a regular polygon called an icosagon. Students may be familiar with more common polygons such as quadrilaterals, pentagons, hexagons, and octagons. After reviewing polygons, have students trace a circle on a sheet of paper. Using their circle as guide, have students use a ruler to draw 20 straight lines (all the same length) around the circle to create a diagram of the Globe Theatre. This will be difficult. Now give students a protractor and inform them that where each line meets another, an inside angle is formed. Each angle of the Globe Theater was exactly 162 degrees. Have students repeat the activity with the circle, using the protractor as an aid. After students have created their icosagon, they can add details such as spectators, a stage, and costumed actors.

Shakespeare's Voice (Language Arts)

In his lifetime of writing, William Shakespeare invented more than 2,000 words and phrases, many of which we use today. List some of these words and phrases on the chalkboard. (Check the glossary in the back of *Stage Fright on a Summer Night.*) Which ones do children recognize? Which are less familiar? Invite students to team up to write a mini-play based on life in the classroom, incorporating some of Shakespeare's language. Students can perform their Shakespearean plays as Readers Theater.

That's Entertainment! (Social Studies)

Jack and Annie learn about the art of theater when they meet William Shakespeare and take part in his play. Have students read through the book and pick out facts about the theater—for example: a performance cost only one cent; men had to play all of the parts; actors read from scripts of rolled-up paper; plays could only be performed in the daytime hours. Make a large Venn diagram on the chalkboard to compare modern-day plays to those of Shakespeare's time.

Good Morning, Gorillas

Before You Read

As Jack and Annie travel to the African rain forest, they meet a group of gorillas. They learn how gorillas behave, what they eat, and how they communicate—without any words, of course. Ask students how they sometimes communicate without using words. Let students take turns demonstrating some examples, such as giving a thumbs-up sign to say "Good job!"

After You Read

Cloud in a Bottle

(Science)

Annie and Jack travel to a rain forest in central Africa. It is called a "cloud forest" because it is up so high in the mountains. Make a cloud forest in the classroom.

- Fill a 2-liter bottle with 1/3 cup hot water. Tape a sheet of black paper behind the bottle.

- Light a match (teacher only), and drop it in the bottle. Immediately cover the container with a small bag of ice. What do students observe in the bottle? (*A cloud will form. The black paper makes it easier to see.*)

- Ask students how they think the cloud formed. Explain that the warm water evaporated and then condensed when it cooled. Condensation causes drops to form on small particles of dust (such as smoke from the match). All of the drops together form a cloud.

Silverback "Scaling"

(Math)

Jack learns that a silverback gorilla is called a "shy and gentle giant." Ask students why the word *giant* fits this gorilla. (*It can weigh 450 pounds.*) To give students a sense of this size, ask: "Do you think all of your backpacks together will weigh more or less than a silverback?" Let children guess and then take turns weighing their backpacks. Do children collectively carry around the weight of a gorilla? If the backpacks weigh less than the gorilla, estimate how many more backpacks would equal 450 pounds. Decide on a way to check these estimates—for example, if a child guesses 10 more backpacks, find the average weight of a backpack, multiply that times 10, and add this number to the previous total.

Learning Sign Language (Language Arts)

Jack and Annie show the gorillas how to say "I love you" in American Sign Language. In 1972, researchers began to teach sign language to a gorilla named Koko, who learned several hundred signs and used them to communicate. Let students practice communicating with signs. Share a book that introduces sign language, such as *You Can Learn Sign Language* by Jackie Kramer and Tali Ovavdia (Troll, 2000). Notice that some hand motions look like the objects or actions they represent. Divide the class into small groups. Have each group develop a sign for something and teach it to the class. Students can practice using their signs to communicate.

Thanksgiving on Thursday

Jack and Annie find themselves back in 1621 for the first Thanksgiving in Plymouth. They try to help prepare for the big feast, but are not familiar with the Pilgrims' ways. Ask students to suggest Thanksgiving traditions and keep these in mind as they read the story. Do any of these traditions match those in the story? What new traditions do they learn?

Fishy Corn

(Science and Language Arts)

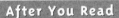

Squanto shows Jack and Annie how to plant corn by "digging a hole and putting two rotting fish in each hole." The fish fertilizes the soil. To investigate how this works, divide the class into small groups. Each group will need potting soil, two small paper cups, seeds (use sweet corn or field corn seeds), and fish emulsion fertilizer. (Check garden supply or home improvement stores for this. Follow instructions for handling.) Have students fill their containers with soil and plant the seeds. Have students water their seeds regularly, using plain water for one and the same amount of water plus fish emulsion fertilizer for the other. Have students record observations in a journal and discuss results. (*The fertilizer gives the plants extra nutrients so their growth has an appreciable difference when compared to the unfertilized plants.*)

Thanksgiving News

(Language Arts)

Priscilla, Squanto, Governor Bradford, and the people of Plymouth show Jack and Annie many interesting things about the Pilgrim way of life. Focus on the facts by having students write or deliver short "news" stories. Share several short, age-appropriate news stories to model the activity. For each, look for answers to who, what, when, where, and why. Let children answer the same questions in their news stories—for example, as they report on the *Mayflower*'s voyage, the peace treaty that Squanto helped negotiate, or a day in the life of a Pilgrim child.

Travel Dictionary

(Language Arts and Social Studies)

"What art…would thou…art thou…" This book is full of unfamiliar ways of speaking. Send students on a scavenger hunt to find more examples. Have them pay particular attention to Priscilla's words. Ask children to write down the sentences they find that use words such as *art*, *thou*, and *thee*. Invite children to provide the translations for each example they find. Together, write a travel dictionary Jack and Annie might have taken back in time with them to the first Thanksgiving. Include words they'd need to know to communicate with the Pilgrims. Since travel dictionaries are often pocket-sized, students can work on small sheets of paper, too.

High Tide in Hawaii

Before You Read

Invite students to explore the history of the Hawaiian Islands by making a picture time line. Using the information at the back of the book or other resources, list some main events in Hawaii's history. For example:

● The Hawaiian Islands were formed millions of years ago when volcanoes rose from the Pacific Ocean.

● The Hawaiian Islands were settled by the Polynesians about 1,500 years ago.

● Hawaii became a state in 1959.

Divide the class into small groups. Give each group a time period and a large sheet of construction paper. Have groups illustrate that time in Hawaii's history. Display the time line as a backdrop for reading the book.

After You Read

Tell a Hula Story
(Movement and Language Arts)

Jack and Annie discover the art of hula dancing while visiting a village in Old Hawaii. Jack reads in his book that because early Hawaiians had no written language, they used dancing and chanting to tell stories. Invite students to create a hula dance to communicate a message. This can be done as a variation on the game Charades. First, have students come up with a message to share with the class. Give students time to practice movements that communicate the message. Let students take turns performing their dances as the class tries to guess the message.

Making Connections
(Language Arts)

High Tide in Hawaii is filled with many natural connections to other books in the Magic Tree House series. For example, the way Hawaiians use dancing to communicate may remind students of the nonverbal communication of the gorillas in *Good Morning, Gorillas.* The geography of the Hawaiian Islands may remind them of what they learned about volcanoes in *Vacation Under the Volcano.* Record connections like these on chart paper. Making connections from one book to another encourages children to revisit stories they've read, make comparisons, and deepen understanding.

Compound-Word Flap Book (Language Arts)

Jack and Annie find their last clue by putting two words together: *friend + ship = friendship.* Invite students to find other words in the book that are like the word *friendship*—for example, *rooftops, backpack,* and *sunlight.* Explain that these words are called compound words and that they are formed by putting two words together to create a new word with a different meaning. Have students make a flap book to practice using compound words:

● Fold a sheet of paper into three equal sections horizontally. The two outside pieces will be folded in over the middle piece.

● Draw a picture of the first part of one word on the left flap and the second part of the word on the right flap. Open the flaps and draw a picture of both words together.

● Trade papers. Look at the outside flaps and try to guess the compound word on the inside.